THE LIGHTNING BOYS 2

For Marcus, Chloe, Leo, Katie, Charlotte, James, Athena and Emily.
Also in memory of Lily.

CONTENTS

INTRODUCTION

Submissions for this book have been sent to me in a variety of formats including diary entries, interviews, notes, log book extracts and audio tapes. As in the first *Lightning Boys*, therefore, every chapter has been written by me although I have used the first person singular throughout and obtained each person's approval before finalising a script. I'd like to thank warmly all of those who showed such illuminating co-operation as the book progressed.

With particular thanks to aviation artist and former Lightning commanding officer Chris Stone who painted the picture on the front jacket cover specially for *Lightning Boys 2*.

Richard Pike
Aberdeenshire, Scotland – 2013

CHAPTER 1

RED ALERT

Steve Gyles by 11(F) Squadron Lightning Mk 6 fitted with over-wing fuel tanks, March 1970.

HOW STEVE GYLES SAVED THE WORLD

It is a truth universally acknowledged that fighter pilots are bold, dedicated individuals of the highest calibre and probity. Despite this general recognition of polymaths with legendary qualities of sophistication, prepossession and perspicacity, some folk may not realise that up there, up at thirty-something thousand odd (sometimes very odd) feet, even a fighter pilot can be left feeling alone and fragile. While, normally, the exhilaration of flying an aircraft such as the Lightning would cause worldly issues to be transcended, situations could arise which might mean that even the finest and fieriest of fighter pilot will be brought down to earth in a most unexpected manner.

Take, for example, the mass arrival in one's vicinity of enemy aircraft in their seemingly endless hordes. When the sky suddenly becomes thick with hostile machinery, when you are outrageously outnumbered and inadequately equipped to do what you are supposed to do, the result is not a happy feeling. I know this because, as happened to the Spitfire and Hurricane pilots in the Battle of Britain, I experienced a similar effect myself some thirty years on from

THE LIGHTNING BOYS 2

TRUE TALES FROM PILOTS AND ENGINEERS OF THE RAF'S ICONIC SUPERSONIC FIGHTER

RICHARD PIKE

Grub Street • London

Published by
Grub Street
4 Rainham Close
London
SW11 6SS

A CIP record for this title is available from the British Library

ISBN-13: 9781909166134

Cover design by Sarah Driver based on a painting by Chris Stone
Formatted by Sarah Driver

Printed and bound by MPG Printgroup Ltd.

Grub Street Publishing only uses
FSC (Forest Stewardship Council) paper for its books.

PUBLISHER'S THANKS

To all contributors and, as always, the indefatigable
and ever helpful Ed Durham.
www.lightningpilots.com

those dark days of 1940. The hollow sensation that strikes the pit of the stomach, the realisation in one awesome, spine-chilling second that you are about to be wholly and dreadfully overwhelmed, is something that has to be gone through to be understood.

As a first tourist at the time, my experience was probably all the more difficult to manage. Recent circumstances had not helped either. Just the previous month, in early March 1970, I had been in the officers' mess at RAF Leuchars in Scotland, the base for my squadron (No 11[F]), when the abrupt, eerie shriek of the station crash alarm had caused all to fall silent and to listen out for further details. After a pause, a terse voice on the Tannoy system announced the news of an off-base crash. At once, I dressed quickly (I'd been in the bath) and hastened to my squadron operations set-up. There, I learnt that one of our pilots, the squadron weapons instructor, had ejected from his Lightning after a double reheat fire by the Isle of May in the Firth of Forth, north of Edinburgh. There was little we could do at that point except pace the room while we awaited information from the search and rescue services. This was slow in coming and everyone became increasingly concerned as the night wore on.

Our worries were reinforced by thoughts of just a few days before when squadron pilots had been required to attend a briefing on safety drills. While attentive to the drills, nevertheless it was hard sometimes to avoid a sense that such drills were, to a degree, hypothetical – a necessary part of training though in reality we might have thought: "This isn't going to happen to me – no way!"

I could recall clearly how, as he had sat on a window ledge that day and as he had stared impatiently outside, our squadron weapons instructor had seemed to reflect that attitude more keenly than most.

This made the situation even more poignant when, finally, we heard that, having survived his ejection, our colleague had died of exposure in the Firth of Forth. He had failed to board his one-man dinghy and a lanyard connecting pilot to dinghy had been found floating in the water some distance away.

Later, we learned some painful facts. Our squadron weapons instructor, we were told, had modified his immersion flying suit by cutting off the watertight, if uncomfortable, rubber boots to replace them with flexible rubber wrist seals. He then had worn ordinary boots and socks – socks which he'd tucked inside the rubber seals; socks, therefore, which had acted like wicks when immersed in the sea. Under his flying suit he had donned a flimsy T-shirt (he'd played a game of squash shortly before flying and consequently had felt hot) thus he had little in the way of thermal insulation. His emergency procedures had been incorrect: instead of activating the 'SARBE' location device he had removed the battery by mistake. Furthermore, his emergency light had been improperly operated as a result of which he had very little illumination and then for a short period only.

Numerous equipment and procedural changes were instituted after this accident. However, of the lessons learned, perhaps the most tragic was the realisation that, if complacency had compounded the various factors which had led to the needless loss of a young, talented life, then not one of us, surely, could claim to be guilt free.

All of this, naturally, was at the forefront of my mind when, the day after the tragedy, I led the first pair of our squadron's Lightnings to fly following the accident. Meanwhile, fire integrity checks were conducted on our aircraft, including those recalled from a detachment to North Wales for missile firing practice. When these checks were completed, another squadron pilot and myself were sent back to North Wales in order to fire off all five of the Red Top air-to-air missiles allocated to the squadron for practice firings. We managed to achieve one firing each before another urgent call ordered us back to Leuchars immediately. Trouble, it seemed, was brewing left, right and centre. The Soviets had decided, evidently, to show off their air power in order to mark the centenary of the birth on 22 April 1870 of their hero Comrade Vladimir Lenin, the gremlin in the Kremlin who, in his time, had managed to out-communist other communists to an amazing extent and who had led the October Revolution of 1917.

From our squadron's perspective, this meant intense periods of duty in the QRA (Quick Reaction Alert) hangar. I was heavily involved, of course, and by mid-April 1970, having completed over half-a-dozen sessions of 24-hour QRA duty during the month, I had begun to feel rather jaded. Aircraft recognition sessions, a regular part of squadron training, featured prominently as we honed our ability to recognise and classify Soviet aircraft. The likes of the four turboprop-engined Tupolev Tu-95, especially the six or seven crew Tu-95 RT version (that veritable icon of the Cold War and code-named Bear D by NATO) and the twin jet-engined Tupolev Tu-16 (code-named Badger) had to be identified from every conceivable angle and under all kinds of lighting conditions.

We were briefed on the limitations of Soviet aircraft, some of which carried political officers on flights. The Russian psyche, it was suggested, was inclined towards violence as a first rather than a last resort, though such ideas tended to be a little over-generalised. "In Russia," someone sensible was supposed to have said one time, "we have no roads, only directions."

For the night of 22/23rd April 1970 I was back on QRA duty. All was tranquil initially as we waited for the possible call to action. The other pilot and I read magazines, watched TV, talked about squadron life. The hour, I believe, was between eleven and midnight when I decided to have a last check of my Lightning before I went to bed. Pilots on QRA duty were allowed to sleep as long as they remained in flying gear. It could seem odd climbing into a bed, freshly made with clean white sheets starched to strict military standards, while still fully dressed in flying kit and boots. However, rules were rules and, like it or not, procedures had to be followed.

It was in the small hours of the morning, at around 0400, that I awoke with a start. An inconspicuous-looking 'squawk' box in one corner of the pilots' crew room had started to make strange sounds. At once, I tumbled out of bed and dashed over to listen closely. A detached voice now reverberated from the box: "*Leuchars, Leuchars, this is Buchan...alert two Lightnings.*"

I shook my head and stared momentarily at the other pilot. He looked as bleary-eyed as I felt. Nevertheless, as the nominated Q1 (the first to go in the event of a scramble order) he ran with admirable élan out to his aircraft. As the Q2 pilot I set off the scramble alarm, acknowledged the Buchan controller's call, scribbled down the time, then sprinted to my Lightning. Both pilots sat in their individual cockpits for a brief period before the controller's voice crackled through our headsets; without ceremony, he ordered the Q1 Lightning to scramble.

A wall separated the two Lightnings but I could hear the familiar racket as my fellow pilot went through his engine start routine. The well-drilled ground crewmen now had to scurry here and there, reposition fire extinguishers, plug in this connector, unplug that one, take away wheel chocks, and monitor the aircraft for signs of leaks or other problems. If, to the untrained eye, the process looked harum-scarum, this was deceptive; in truth, every man knew exactly what was required of him and the procedures were slick and professional.

When my colleague was safely airborne, the controller stood me down from cockpit readiness. By now too worked-up to think of going back to sleep, I made myself a cuppa and sat quietly in the crew room to await developments. Developments soon began to develop. Before long, I was aware of frenetic activity as squadron personnel were summoned to their places of duty. Matters, it appeared, were getting serious. Soon, surrounding hustle and bustle became increasingly hectic as more Lightnings were prepared for QRA back-up duties. Meanwhile, a series of conversations with the Buchan controller kept me up-to-date with the overall scenario.

It was just as dawn was breaking that my colleague returned. The urbane, pipe-smoking pilot, Alan White, remained characteristically unflustered as he described how, in pretty much pitch-black conditions, he had shadowed two Soviet bombers – Bear D aircraft, he reckoned. Too preoccupied to think carefully about the fighter pilot's general reputation for probity, sophistication, prepossession and perspicacity, nonetheless I could not avoid a sense of admiration for the way he had handled a most demanding and hazardous situation. Any such reflections, however, had to be put aside when the 'squawk' box abruptly came to life once more.

"Leuchars, this is Buchan," the controller sounded a bit breathless this time, "alert two Lightnings." A small but significant hesitation ensued before, most unusually, he continued: "and as many more as you can manage." The controller's tone then became almost plaintive as he went on: "we have eighty plus unidentified tracks coming round the North Cape."

I gazed for a second or two at the whites of White's cold blue eyes. We said nothing but our thoughts seemed to coincide: eighty plus? Is he mad? Have we gone back to Battle of Britain days? Has World War Three broken out? Further mental machinations, though, had to be swiftly abandoned as we set off the scramble alarm and I made a dash for my Lightning (the 'Q1' aircraft was in the process of engineering turn-round and the 'Q3' back-up was still being prepared for flight).

My judiciously placed headset (otherwise known as 'bone dome'), efficaciously laid-out cape leather flying gloves, and thoughtfully positioned seat straps facilitated speedy progress as I leapt into the cockpit, plugged in my PEC (personal equipment connector) and buckled up the seat straps. Within a remarkably short period of time I was ready to fly. This was fortuitous. The Buchan controller now gave height, heading and a few other details as he ordered me to scramble and to maintain radio silence. My God, I thought, perhaps this really is war.

My start-up procedures went without hitches and before long, as I taxied towards the runway, the air traffic controller, in compliance with Buchan's 'radio silence' order, shone a bright green light in my direction as a means of indicating take-off clearance. A hasty glance around the cockpit confirmed that all pre-take-off checks had been completed. Without further ado I advanced both throttles to the full cold power position, allowed the engines to settle for a moment or two, then eased the throttles leftwards and forwards to select full reheat. The twin Rolls-Royce Avon engines responded with their customary panache and within seconds my peripheral vision picked up a blur of runway lights on either side as the Lightning accelerated.

Pale shafts of dawn sunlight began to emerge across the area as I climbed.

I was still required to keep radio silence but my lone situation somehow felt even more alone than normal, especially in view of the circumstances. My airborne radar, my navigational aids, the 'identification friend or foe' system – all had to be switched off to thwart the possibility of tactical information being passed on by eavesdroppers. My task, consequently, amounted to flying the Lightning while I kept a good look-out for other aircraft as, simultaneously, I maintained a mental navigational plot – in other words back to the good old-fashioned techniques of Tiger Moth days (even if the aeroplane itself was somewhat souped-up).

As I headed north-east, the distinctive outline of the mainland of Scotland soon disappeared behind me. However, with regular time/speed calculations I could work out a navigational plot with reasonable accuracy. From time to time this could be verified by peering down at fixed-position North Sea oil installations. I had been airborne for a little over thirty minutes or so when I reckoned to be approaching the general area briefed by the Buchan controller in his scramble instructions. It was about time, I thought, to break radio silence. I glanced inside the cockpit as I switched on the 'identification friend or foe' system, the navigational aids and the AI23B airborne radar. The radar took some moments to warm up but when it had done so, and when I squinted through the fold-up rubber viewing shade of the radar's B-scope cockpit display, what I saw made my pulse start to race and my brain cells go into overdrive. The radar revealed mass contacts too numerous to count up. I had expected something unusual but this was overwhelming; I struggled to absorb the ramifications; my heart seemed displaced to the area of my solar plexus and my throat felt deprived of breath. Indeed, I became so engrossed that I almost forgot to breathe. I felt like a solitary matador (not that I have ever attempted bullfighting) confronted with not one but with – who knows? – 60...70...80 plus raging creatures all bent on widespread death and destruction.

The mass contacts, within a range of twenty to sixty miles from my position, persisted to march towards me. I spoke to the controller at RAF Saxa Vord, a ground radar unit on the northern tip of the Shetland Islands, who verified that my airborne radar information was correct. "Copied," I tried to sound nonchalant and James Bond-like but my voice, annoyingly, had become shrill. I swallowed hard and wondered what the hell to do next. However, in a way, the dilemma was resolved for me when, quite soon, I visually spotted the first wave of Soviet aircraft. From this moment, more or less, my radar became redundant as I concentrated on the visual picture outside my cockpit.

It appeared that the Soviet hordes, mainly Badger and Bear aircraft, had organised themselves into groups of finger-four formation. With somewhat preternatural concepts swirling through my head, I selected a likely-looking group and manoeuvred my Lightning for an interception and visident (visual identification) procedure. Normally, in this situation (commonly described as cat-and-mouse) I was supposed, presumably, to represent the cat. However, on this day I could not avoid a disagreeable sense of role reversal. I was armed with two live missiles to defend our homeland, but my opponents were armed on a rather larger scale. Their load of nuclear bombs and missiles, horrific weaponry able to trigger global holocaust and at the root of the relentless Cold War, were weapons which could make my couple of air-to-air missiles seem kind of puny. For me in my lone Lightning, the implications could hardly have been greater; one false move and the possible hiatus was best not imagined.

My nerves, as might be expected, were on edge while I closed up on the potentially hostile formation. I needed to exercise caution but not to the exclusion of the efficient conduct of my task. With the ephemeral nature of this situation, and conscious of the precariousness of the ephemeral, every move appeared to assume excessive significance. As I drew ever closer to the Soviet machines I knew that I had to keep a cool head. By now I had identified them as Tu-16 Badgers and it was time to take photographs. I had been supplied with a special 35mm camera with an automatic wind-on facility and plenty of film. I moved up to the rear of the formation, took a photograph of both sides and underneath Badger number four, then moved on to the next machine.

I had just completed my photo shoot of the formation's third Badger when my peripheral vision picked up a shadow passing over the Lightning's cockpit. At once I glanced up to see another formation of four Badgers cross about 500 feet above me. This seemed suddenly to emphasise the surreal nature of what was happening around me; it was as if I had been caught up in some crazy dream; maybe I needed to pinch myself to return to reality. A small voice within me whispered, "well I'll be darned".

At about this time the Saxa Vord controller advised me that a Victor air-to-air refuelling tanker was in the vicinity. I therefore asked the controller for 'pigeons' (heading and distance) to the tanker to which he replied: "I haven't got a clue. There are 60 or more contacts in close proximity and all are heading south-west."

"All heading south-west?"

"Yes, all of them."

I hesitated for a moment then spoke directly to the Victor tanker crew: "request you turn through 180 degrees for identification."

"Wait one," replied the Victor's captain. "We're in the process of intercepting three Soviet Bears."

I had to smile...yes!...at these words which, so unexpectedly, gave me a welcome fillip. I admired the captain's initiative even if my ongoing sense of the other-worldly had been underscored. We'll make a fighter pilot out of you yet, I thought. Later, though, I heard that the air vice-marshal in charge of the Victors had adopted a different attitude. He was furious, so I heard, and far from congratulating his men, he had reacted with unfortunate Bomber Command-type mentality. In future, he decreed, Victor tankers would be banned from flying within ten miles of Soviet aircraft. Oh dear, I thought, how would the good air vice-marshal cope with the tough realities of grim, all-out war? Perhaps, like rather too many, the fellow was overly focussed on his peacetime career.

When, eventually, the Victor captain had carried out the necessary turn, I was able quickly to identify the tanker amongst the mass of other radar returns. I advanced my throttles to overtake the Soviet formations as I headed towards the Victor. My in-flight refuel, which proceeded without difficulty, filled my aircraft's tanks to full and soon I was able to leave the Victor and return to the fray where I was joined by another Lightning.

For the next one-and-a-half hours, as I moved from one formation to the next, I was able to photograph proceedings for posterity. The situation was unique, and I knew it. Never had we seen such masses before and never were we likely to do so again. The reaction of Soviet crews was intriguing: some would studiously ignore us and these Bears and Badgers, I assumed, had political observers on board. Crews on the non-political machines seemed to react altogether differently – almost festively – when chicken legs, drink cans, maybe even the odd tumbler of vodka were waved around merrily. After all, I reminded myself, this was supposed to be some kind of weird birthday bash. If, from time to time, I asked Saxa Vord for pigeons to base, some of the Soviet crews would helpfully hold a map against one of their side windows and point. As my initial worries progressively softened – almost, but not quite, to the extent of becoming rather flabby – eventually the time came for both Lightnings to leave the party and return to base.

En route to Leuchars the Victor captain called us on the radio to say that he was currently flying in company with a Bear D. "I've run out of photographic film," he said, "have you any left?"

"No problem," we said and altered heading to rendezvous with the spontaneously formed, if highly unconventional, formation. It was these photographs that appeared in the national press the next day (see picture section).

And it was the next day, as I sat in the officers' mess anteroom thumbing through the pages of the *Daily Telegraph*, that I came across a copy of one of my pictures adjacent to an article which finished with the words: '*...Strike Command pilots are becoming adept at "Bear hunting" and although unable to communicate with the Russian aircrews appropriate hand signals are invariably exchanged.*'

I began to appreciate then that, despite initial trepidation stirred up by unknown factors, I had been placed in an exceptional position and, in an odd sort of way, an exceptionally fortunate position. I had witnessed history in the making. With ten Soviet aircraft interceptions on that day (by the time of my retirement from the service in 1990 the overall number had increased to 35), seven by my fellow Lightning pilot, Graham Clarke, and three by the bold if soon-to-be-barred Victor crew, I believe that we achieved a record. Furthermore, my sense of satisfaction was strengthened when I thought about what lay ahead in the not-too-distant future.

"You're a jammy bastard," I advised myself eventually. "You're getting married next month but first you had to save the world. Two life-changing events within weeks of each other. You jammy, lucky so-and-so." I knew, of course, that there were two people inside me – the fighter pilot and the fiancé – both of whom, for better or worse, required qualities of probity, prepossession and perspicacity and both of whom, for rather diverse reasons, remained stoically on red alert.

CHAPTER 2

STORMY STRUGGLE

56(F) Squadron Lightning flies over Cyprus.

RAINDROPS KEPT FALLING ON ROGER COLEBROOK'S HEAD

With a sense of awkwardness I stared up at the briefing room ceiling. The briefing officer, interrupted by the increasing racket of rain that drummed incessantly on the flimsy roof, gazed at me. He remained silent for some moments and in the ensuing pause I made cracks in the corrugations turn into charts of roads and hills, and I wondered how much more this rickety prefabricated structure could endure before drips of water turned into disastrous deluges. I speculated on whether the night-time flight we were planning would be realistic in these drastic conditions. As if he had read my mind, the briefing officer raised his voice to continue.

"Sod it," said Squadron Leader Paul Hobley, who, as well as leader for the planned sortie, was my 56(F) Squadron flight commander. A humorous man, our flight commander was no ectomorph. His buoyant, larger-than-life character offered a role model for the younger pilots like myself. "We're meant to be an all-weather outfit, are we not?" He looked up at the ceiling.

"Yes, sir," I said meekly.

"In that case," he growled, "we should fly in all weather conditions, should we not?"

"That's okay with me."

The flight commander, though, seemed unconvinced by his own line of logic. Perhaps conscious of my lack of flying experience on the Lightning, he appeared to struggle with his necessary decision. He stepped towards the nearest window and squinted his eyes as he tried to look outside. "Bugger," he breathed, as if to himself; his attempts to observe were thwarted by rain driven forcefully against the glass. I guessed that conflicting ideas within his head must have been influenced by the events of just six months ago – the Arab-Israeli Six-Day War had been fought a short distance across the Mediterranean Sea from our squadron base at Akrotiri in Cyprus. At the front of all our minds, the situation remained volatile; our involvement in one way or another could not be ruled out. We had been briefed, for instance, on how, three days into the conflict, on Thursday 8th June 1967, a United States ship, the *USS Liberty*, had been attacked by Israeli jets and torpedo boats. The *Liberty*, very nearly sunk in the assault, had suffered over 30 deaths and many injured sailors. Israeli apologies had been received with scepticism by some US crew members who claimed that the attack, so they reckoned, may well have been deliberate.

If Israel, or another Middle East country, decided to attack Cyprus (which would happen seven years later with the Turkish invasion of the island) then our 56(F) Squadron Lightning Mk 3s would be required to provide air defence of the sovereign base areas. Bearing in mind the Six-Day War, this was some commitment for we had been briefed on how, at 0745 hours (Israeli time) on the morning of 5th June 1967, coincident with civil defence sirens sounding across Israel, all but 12 of the Israeli Air Force's nearly 200 jet aircraft had conducted a mass attack against Egyptian airfields. The Israelis had approached below radar cover and in the ensuing mêlée a total of over 300 Egyptian aircraft, including large numbers of the latest Soviet-built MiG 21 fighters and Tu-16 Badger medium bombers, had been destroyed and some 100 Egyptian pilots killed.

Such a scenario applied to our Cyprus situation with our dozen or so 56(F) Squadron Lightnings would mean that – to put it mildly – we'd face challenges of Gordian knot complexity. We knew that our best tactic, therefore, was to build a reputation as an efficient, audacious unit capable of operating in any weather, day or night, to provide deterrence against attack in this tense and turbulent region. During the Six-Day War, and for a short period afterwards, our QRA (Quick Reaction Alert) duties, normally restricted to daylight hours, were extended to a full 24-hour commitment. Camp beds were set up in the squadron crew room and rostered pilots slept in their flying suits. Pilots were briefed to expect possible defectors from Israel's neighbours who might seek safe haven at Akrotiri. From my own point of view, I was non-operational at the time nevertheless I slept most nights in the squadron crew room in order to provide support in the form of tea, coffee, snacks and general dogs-body tasks for the operational pilots.

"Oh, bloody hell," said the flight commander. His vivid eyes burned forth from plump cheeks as he gazed first at me, then outside. "I think I'll have a word with the engineers."

My mind was in turmoil as I watched him push past the briefing room's cheap, battered furniture towards the telephone. He picked up the receiver and my thoughts seemed to churn. Just over a year had elapsed since my first solo flight on the Lightning and although I felt that I'd matured considerably during that period, I was still only twenty-one years of age and still had much to learn. I had always wanted to be a fighter pilot; I loved flying – even if it meant coping with sub-tropical rain storms from time to time – but I was learning that sometimes the job's realities did not always match dreamy-headed expectations. Demands could be tough in a belligerent world embroiled in hostilities. As well as the ongoing ramifications of the Six-Day War, the Vietnam War was a serious issue at the time. The United States, with hundreds of thousands of troops committed to Vietnam, relied on air superiority and overwhelming fire power to defeat the pro-communist Vietcong guerrillas. Despite this, the war did not appear to be going well for the Americans. We would read in the newspapers about large-scale attacks by the likes of B66 Destroyer aircraft and F105 Thunderchiefs, but we would read, too, about the terrible numbers of casualties suffered by both sides.

"You're joking," the flight commander scowled as he spoke on the phone. "This seems to be a reasonable theoretical statement on the subject," he continued, "but…" I turned to watch as he made a circling gesture with his left hand as if to encourage applause. "Fine," he said, "let's do it that way, then." He replaced the receiver and gazed in my direction. "Well, young Roger," he said, "looks like we're going to fill our boots." He guffawed and went on: "or get them filled, more like."

"Right-oh," I said. I watched him closely as he walked back to his chair and sat down again.

"The engineers want to adopt special procedures in this weather," he said.

"The start-up crews will be wearing heavy oilskins for protection so won't be able to assist with the strapping-in process. The aircraft canopies will be kept closed for as long as practicable, we'll have to open them ourselves then close them ASAP when we're in the cockpits. We'll follow normal procedures from then on. Are you okay with that? Are you happy?"

"Ecstatic!"

"Good-oh." At this, he hastily re-summarised the details of our planned sortie's high altitude work before we both stood up, donned our life jackets and 'bone domes' (headsets) and moved towards the crew room's exit door. For a moment we stood by the open door and listened to the dull, sullen sound of deluge. We glanced at each other, nodded, and began to run.

The distance we had to cover was not great, just a hundred yards or so. Time and motion, however, became distorted as we tried to rush, heads bowed, eyes half-closed, towards the engineering line hut. Wincing at the sting of driving rain against faces, our progress was hampered by impromptu streams that swirled around our feet. More like sailors on deck than airmen about to fly, in our confined world of wind and wet I could almost feel a ship's motion, the scour of flotsam thrown up by the seas, the sting of salt against face and hands. While we struggled onwards, I seemed to hear the creaks and groans of the ship's superstructure, the grumbles and gurgles as spray, solid as streamers, was propelled against us before exhausted remnants careered towards overworked drainage systems. Just as the ship's steering gear would struggle to weave the ship's course, so the flight commander and I threaded our way through the torrents until suddenly, looking like a couple of drowned rats, we burst into the line hut.

The line chief and his men watched us warily. Too polite to make any comment, their expressions nonetheless suggested: "Are you nuts, or something? Are you off your tiny rockers?" We walked towards a desk to check the aircraft logs. "Oh Roger, Roger," I reasoned with myself, "am I nuts? Have I lost the plot? Am I off my jolly little rocker?" I scrawled a signature in the aircraft technical log, saw that the flight commander had done the same, glanced at the line chiefie and noted his continued muteness. Admittedly the flight commander and I with bone domes on our heads could not hear very well, nevertheless it struck me that some comment, perhaps a terse "good luck, gents" or even "goodbye, gents," would not have gone amiss. Silence, though, persisted as we two pilots braced ourselves for another dash.

When, after what felt like an ongoing sea dip, the pair of us eventually reached our aircraft, further problems had to be tackled. In order to operate the

Lightning's perspex canopy, a fiddly side hatch had to be accessed after which, at the press of a switch, the canopy could be hydraulically raised. The procedure, though, appeared painfully long-drawn-out, especially with wet, slippery hands. As speedily as possible I carried out the briefed procedure, scrambling into the cockpit from where I could operate the internal cockpit switch to re-close the canopy. By then, however, the interior of the cockpit, including the Martin Baker ejection seat, had become drenched. There was a puddle of water by my feet. The inside of the canopy had started to mist over. The aircraft instruments, beaded with water, were hard to read. Attempts to mop up with my handkerchief, shirt sleeves, gloves – anything – were hampered as these items were themselves already sodden. I strived, however, to make the best of a bad job as I carried out the pre-start checks. Then, after a glance at the other Lightning, I signalled 'engine start' to the attendant crewman who, planted there in his stiff oilskins, would not have looked out of place on the heaving deck of a square-rigger off Cape Horn. Nevertheless, he returned my hand signal at which I reached for the start buttons and pressed the appropriate one.

Fortunately, the first of the Rolls-Royce Avons fired-up without difficulty – testimony to the engine's reliability in even the foulest of conditions – and I could switch on the Lightning's powerful demisting system. Although the inside of the canopy around my head began to clear, problems at the other end persisted: pools of water by my feet continued to slosh around the floor.

"I'm in an all-weather fighter aircraft...an all-weather fighter aircraft...an all-weather..." the flight commander's edict ran through my head as I monitored the engines' start cycles. With both engines successfully 'burning and turning' I waited for the leader's radio call to air traffic control for taxi clearance. Soon, when this had been granted, we began to make steady progress along the rain-swept taxiways. While we made headway I thought about tonight's contrast to more usual Cypriot weather when, in daytime, heat haze would hang like a vapour over the airfield. A typical day's sun would bear down on shoulders and backs, perspiration would seep from skin, trickle down necks to collect by belts, and prickly heat would cause airforce issue shirts to feel damp and uncomfortable.

However, tonight's damp, caused by rather different reasons, was put swiftly to the back of my mind when the leader was cleared to take off. When he moved to the downwind side of the runway in order to avoid spray and jet-wake blowing across my take-off path, I thought so far so good. As the leader released his aircraft brakes, I pressed the timer on my stopwatch. After 30 seconds, I released my own brakes, selected full cold power (use of reheat in these conditions was not recommended), and held the ailerons into wind as my aircraft set off down the runway. My peripheral vision picked up a spray-filled blur of runway lights on each side as the Lightning accelerated. At the appropriate airspeed I pulled back the stick for lift-off at which point, quite suddenly, I realised that I had a problem. The main attitude indicator on my flight instrument panel, the not-too-catchily-named OR946, had moved promptly to the top of its glass window and flopped onto its side. Furthermore, I had suffered a simultaneous tailplane trim nose-up runaway – I needed to push hard on the stick to retain control of the aircraft.

In these conditions I relied heavily on my flight instruments to indicate the aircraft heading and attitude. Unless I knew instantly whether I was in a climb, a descent or a turn, disorientation and potential disaster would follow rapidly. The standby horizon still functioned but, tiny and awkwardly placed, this was an instrument of last resort. With low cloud scudding around at some 300 feet I reckoned that my safest option was to stay below this level. Without looking, I fumbled around in the cockpit to feel for the autopilot master switch and the stability augmentation switch. I turned them off but this had no effect. I made an emergency call to air traffic control. Just as the controller responded, the attitude indicator on the said OR946 immediately reversed its position and the aircraft pitched nose-down. At once, my push on the control stick had to be converted to an anguished pull to prevent a frenetic earthwards plunge. Fortunately this worked, but as I raised the aircraft nose, the tailplane trim now ran fully nose-up again. In a split-second my desperate pull on the stick had to revert once more to an equally desperate, adrenaline-charged push.

"Shit," I thought as, with high anxiety, I attempted to assess my situation. At least I could see a pattern now: an aircraft climbing attitude induced runaway nose-up trim, and vice-versa. In other words, anything other than a straight and level attitude would mean trouble. I decided not to raise the undercarriage and, consequently, I had to keep my airspeed below the 250 knot undercarriage limiting speed. I decided also that, come what may, I should not lose sight of the yellow glow from station and married quarter lighting which was eerily, but fortuitously, reflected along the base of the low cloud. My best hope was to fly as judiciously as possible and attempt to keep aircraft movements in pitch to the minimum. I reasoned, too, that a push force would be required as the aircraft nose came up for the final part of the approach.

As I turned the Lightning downwind I knew that fine judgement was required: a circuit that was wide enough to offer room for manoeuvre, but one that was not too wide – not too much of a Bomber Command-type effort that might cause me to lose sight of the airfield lights. At what I reckoned to be a suitable moment, I lowered the flaps and began to ease the airspeed back to 185 knots. As I did so, I noted that, with the flaps down, the aircraft's vertical oscillations seemed to reduce. I double-checked the cockpit 'three wheels' indicator to confirm that the undercarriage was down and then, still guided by the reflected yellow glow from surrounding cloud, I turned the aircraft onto final approach. Despite the persistent, prodigious downpour of rain, the Lightning's powerful rain dispersal system, with air from the engines' mighty compressors blasted directly at the windshield base, meant that I was able to see the runway lights slip into view while I turned. As I lined the machine up with the runway, I extended the airbrakes to help ease my airspeed back from 185 knots towards 165 knots.

Now, as expected, I was conscious of the growing push force required on the stick. Gradually, with deliberate, measured increases of push force, I started to ease the Lightning down...*200 feet...watch it, Roger, anticipate the crosswind...150 feet...concentrate on a good approach angle...100 feet...maintain that forward push force and keep those wings level...50 feet...the threshold's rushing towards you now...look well ahead...*

Suddenly I felt a thump as the Lightning touched down firmly just beyond the runway threshold. At once, I closed both throttles, pushed the stick as far forward as I could manage, and operated the tail 'chute mechanism. An immediate jerk signified that the tail parachute had deployed. Now, at last, with sensations of elation and relief in roughly equal parts, I knew that I had the machine under control. The landing, less than ceremonious, had worked out okay – an unconventional three-pointer with the main wheels and nose-wheel touching down simultaneously – but never mind, I thought, at least the machine was down, the aircraft had been saved, a Martin Baker let-down (use of my Martin Baker ejection seat) had been avoided.

It was not until the next day, when the engineers had examined my aircraft, Lightning XP755, that they were able to explain what had gone wrong. An electrical junction box, mounted on the cockpit floor, had ingested water during the night's storms. When the aircraft nose was raised or lowered, water ran to the front or rear of the junction box thus shorting-out terminals connected to the OR946 system and to the tailplane trim.

At the time, however, I merely felt continued relief at the way things had worked out. Eventually, when my flight commander landed, we decided that, without further ado, we should drive across to the flight catering section for our night-flying supper.

When we reached the small dining room, and while the flight commander went to order our night-flying meals, I walked over to an adjacent window. I looked out wistfully at the soaking, semi-tropical scene. The approach road, normally well-used, was wind-swept and deserted. Raindrops glistened on plant leaves; thick, silvery spots of reflected light, like weighty beads of mercury. The dining room's windows rattled ominously in the callous wind. While I pondered the night's whole bizarre episode, the world's worries appeared heavy on my shoulders. Even the timing had seemed portentous: I had passed my first green instrument rating test that very morning; before today I would not have been qualified to fly in these conditions.

If my mood was becoming morose, the sound of my flight commander's spontaneous laughter swiftly cheered me up. I took a deep breath, turned around, and began to walk towards the dining table. It was not long before I picked up the smell of cured bacon cooked, no doubt, on an over-worked frying pan. "Manna," I thought, "absolute manna. Fit for the gods." Suddenly I knew that our night-flying supper that evening would be not only hard-earned but even more delicious than usual. I knew that it would help me, too, to keep a sense of proportion over exaggerated worries stirred up in my head by the anomalous nature of the night's stormy struggle.

CHAPTER 3

MAGICAL MYSTERY TOURS

Bill Maish, Don Brown, and Dave Ligget shaking hands with a visitor (unknown) to 74(F) Squadron, RAF Leuchars, Scotland.

DON BROWN REMEMBERS A SEMINAL YEAR

'TIGER' SQUADRONS MEET AT LEUCHARS, 1966

To observers on the ground it must have looked spectacular. It might even have looked spectacularly odd. People might have scratched their heads in wonder when five Lightnings, as they manoeuvred in neat, close formation positions on a fine July morning over quiet countryside near the River Tay in Scotland, suddenly should start to scatter in all directions like demented, startled rabbits. Watchers might have speculated, too, on what could have caused the lead aircraft to appear, quite promptly, to go mad. The episode occurred during our 74(F) Squadron work-up for a NATO 'Tiger Meet' at RAF Leuchars, Fife.

Earlier, we had been briefed on a careful series of manoeuvres designed to be flown later that week over Leuchars airfield. Before the display itself, when we practised our routines away from the airfield, we were keen to work up to a standard that would out-Red Arrow the Red Arrows. The display, we knew, would be viewed with critical eyes by fellow pilots. We would have to offer something special in order to impress the assembled Tiger Meet guests.

We aimed to co-ordinate our formation moves with those of the squadron aerobatics display pilot. For one of the manoeuvres the solo aerobatic man, as he led the other four Lightnings in a thunderous flypast across the airfield, would perform a sudden so-called twinkle roll while the rest of us maintained station. "It should be no problem," the solo aerobatic man, Dave Liggett, had assured us, "my twinkle roll will take up no space at all." At the due moment, however, when he called: "*rolling...now*," his subsequent twinkle roll had taken up, in fact, a considerable amount of twinkle. The manoeuvre also had reduced his airspeed to a level well below that of the other aircraft. We should have anticipated this, of course, but we did not and as a consequence the other pilots, including myself as number four in the planned 'box' formation, became instantly convinced of imminent collision. While the rest of us scattered to the four winds, the solo aerobatic man was left well and truly solo.

It took some time, not to mention agitated radio calls, for us to find each other again, but eventually the somewhat embarrassed team members re-formed for another attempt. With further practice and a fair amount of percipience, we managed to refine the manoeuvre which worked well on the day itself.

The Tiger Meet was an international affair initiated five years earlier, in 1961. The original concept, which began when three squadrons with a tiger as their unit emblem had decided to meet up, had grown in popularity. By 1966 the number of participants had swelled to eight squadrons when units from Belgium, Canada, France, West Germany, the UK and the USA provided an intriguing mix of experienced operators of various aircraft types. Crews flew in each others' dual aircraft, combat sorties between different aircraft types were flown, exchanges of ideas flowed, and discussions about operational procedures and tactics enhanced our common competence. One time, for example, when 'attacked' by two Lightning F3s, three Super Mystère pilots were astonished by their opponents' ability to accelerate and climb into the attack.

The common language was English yet the diversity of accents was eclectic. After-work conversations in messes and bars were revealing. "Never even saw the sonnavabitch...came at me right out of the sun..." "Too bad, huh?" – this with a Gallic shrug – "*C'est la guerre, non*?" "For you ze war is over..." one of our tame squadron pilots (the tactful one) chatted with a new-found German friend.

At one point, with guests treated to the wail of Scottish bagpipes, the parley eased as attention was diverted. The sounds of bagpipes, no doubt not to the

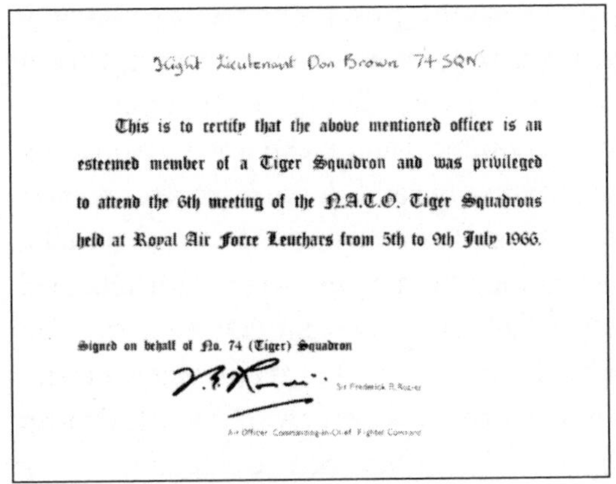

Flight Lieutenant Don Brown 74 SQN.

This is to certify that the above mentioned officer is an esteemed member of a Tiger Squadron and was privileged to attend the 6th meeting of the N.A.T.O. Tiger Squadrons held at Royal Air Force Leuchars from 5th to 9th July 1966.

Signed on behalf of No. 74 (Tiger) Squadron

Sir Frederick R. Rosier

Air Officer Commanding-in-Chief Fighter Command

Don Brown's Tiger Meet certificate.

taste of all, nonetheless appeared to induce heady emotions. The curious acoustics of the hills and mountains seemed to carry the tunes to distant parts. I glanced at the faces of the different nationalities. I imagined Canadian Mounties, American apple pie, Belgian *chocolat*, German *bratwurst*, French *baguette*. We fed them, of course, with Scottish haggis.

Bonhomie may have been bonnie, discussions spirited, attitudes generally relaxed but all of this could give no hint of the tragedy that was to follow.

There were plenty of witnesses when, at around ten in the morning on Friday, 8th July 1966, Capitaine Joel Dancel of the French air force (l'Armée de l'Air) 1/12 Escadron de Chasse took off in a Super Mystère aircraft. The weather was fair that morning and the day's forecast was good, but conscious, perhaps, of the region's fickle climate he had decided to run through his bad weather routine. With an imaginary cloudbase of 500 feet, this involved a series of hard turns and reversals. The Capitaine was an experienced display pilot, he had rehearsed his routine many times before. However, not long after the commencement of his sequence, when in a hard left turn, we watched in stunned silence when the Super Mystère's angle of bank abruptly flicked off. At that instant we were uncertain what might have happened. Doubts were terribly dispelled, though, when the aircraft nose reared up with violence before the aircraft, its wings still level with the horizon, fell earthwards in a fearsome, fatal stall into a field just beyond the airfield boundary.

At the sight of a fireball and at the sound of the airfield crash alarm, some observers' hands immediately went up to cover their mouths in spontaneous gestures of horror. As the haunting tones of the crash alarm faded away, an uncanny hush ensued, broken occasionally by ongoing gasps of astonishment, a few muttered oaths, the movement of emergency vehicles. An officer hastened towards the squadron buildings. Others started to follow though I noticed that one young pilot remained rooted to the spot as if unable to comprehend the full implications of what had happened.

Gradually, however, as brutal truths began to sink in and as gruesome fascination was forced from minds, further activity was prompted. The situation seemed surreal; events proceeded in a blur. I was aware of a lingering sense of detachment from reality. I felt myself recoil with shock – a shock that struck me like a blow in the face. I suffered a complete and inexplicable hearing loss for the period between the first sign of trouble and the sight of the fireball. I perceived the hollow pangs of dread in my belly. As if in a dream, I struggled with ethereal thoughts, complexities of human emotions at once dark, charmed, disembodied. I breathed deeply in. I glanced at my hand-held camera. I had tried to take a photo of the Super Mystère in that fatal turn but later, when the film was developed, the aircraft was nowhere to be seen. A second or so earlier and the Super Mystère would have been in the shot; a second or so later and the fireball would have been shown. The accident had been as rapid as it had been calamitous.

Don Brown flies a 'go-around' at the 1966 Tiger Meet at RAF Leuchars, Scotland.

Difficult decisions were now needed urgently. A meeting between the RAF Leuchars station commander and the visiting squadron commanders was hastily summoned. Capitaine Dancel had been a popular man, held in high esteem by his compatriots and others who knew him. Consequently, his squadron colleagues, as well as other members of the Tiger Meet, were of the strong opinion that the air display scheduled for that afternoon should carry on as planned. It would have been, they said, Capitaine Dancel's wish.

That afternoon, therefore, as I flew in my allotted slot as number four in the box formation, my concentration was intense. I was fiercely focussed on the job in hand; our formation efforts, as with the rest of the display – opened by the Spitfire and Hurricane show-stealers of the RAF's prestigious Battle of Britain Memorial Flight – worked well. Everyone applauded; hand-shaking ensued; we heard many words of congratulations. Yet I could not rid my head of what I had so recently witnessed. My bittersweet feelings, I felt sure, were replicated in one way or another in the minds and in the hearts of every person present.

OPERATION MAGIC CARPET

It was just a few months later, when I was seated in the air traffic control tower, that I was overcome by an awful sense of *déjà vu*. "My God," I thought. "Not again."

By then I no longer viewed the green hills of Scotland or listened to the singular squawks of bagpipes. Instead, my outlook was dominated by seemingly endless acres of featureless sand; an outlook which, when seen from an altitude of 35,000 or so feet, looked like vast stretches of crumpled brown paper.

My move to Saudi Arabia had been initiated by a strange-sounding phone call from a strange-sounding gentleman. The fellow claimed that he was a retired group captain who now worked for an outfit called Airwork, but I had not heard of that company, neither had I heard of him. Money, it seemed, was at the root of all his logic.

"Your salary," he said, "will be four or five times greater than the amount you've been earning as a flight lieutenant."

"But I've already got a job lined up," I protested.

"Bet it's nothing to do with Lightnings," he persisted.

"True...I'll be flying airliners with Qantas."

"Huh!" He snorted. "There you are then."

"Where am I, exactly?"

"What I'm offering," he sighed, "is the opportunity to carry on flying Lightnings. You'll be paid a great deal and it'll all be tax free."

I did a few hasty mental calculations. My military gratuity of £1500 would be virtually tripled in a mere six months. With a tidy sum like that I would be in a position to buy a house in East Anglia if I changed my mind about a job with Qantas.

"I'll think about it," I said.

"I'll call you back soon," he said.

True to form, mystery-man called me back very soon. "Yes," I said. "Okay, okay. Have it your own way. Consider me duly bribed."

"That's the idea," he said.

Before I knew it terms had been agreed, a contract period negotiated and in early-August 1966, having bade farewell to my bemused and not-too-happy-about-what-was-going-on wife, I flew out to Riyadh Airport in Saudi Arabia. I was ensconced in American-style bachelor officer quarters at the Royal Saudi Air Force base co-located at the airport, and I was introduced to the others on the 'squadron'. We were a group of five Lightning pilots (Airwork had been contracted to provide six pilots but never managed to achieve the full quota) none of whom, apart from myself, had any previous experience on a Lightning squadron. We were, in short, a motley crew, best described as 'demonstration pilots' to 'show the flag' (the Saudi flag). We would do whatever the Saudis wanted us to do, short of going to war; mercenaries we were not.

It was not long before I was introduced to the wiles and ways of transactions in a Saudi souk. The dress code for women in these public places was severe, even for European and American guests. Despite this, different nationalities made their presence known. The accents were unmistakeable. Sometimes I would feel twinges of nostalgia when I overheard an obviously English voice.

To barter a deal for, say, a small gold bracelet required the hide of a rhinoceros, a brain like a computer and infinite patience. I could not avoid a sense of deep admiration for the man who had negotiated the Saudi Lightning deal. This had necessitated lengthy, mind-boggling haggles between the British Aircraft Corporation, the Ferranti Company, the Bristol Company, the Royal Air Force, the UK government, Airwork and last but by no means least, an esoteric gang of princes from the Kingdom of Saudi Arabia's royal family. The contract included the training of aircrew as well as ground engineers and support personnel, a guided missile air defence system, a radar network and complex infrastructure. The first element of the training programme involved teaching the English language, including thousands of technical terms, to many hundreds of young Saudis. An interim arrangement, code-named 'Operation Magic Carpet', was designed to provide Saudi Arabia with an immediate fast-jet presence during the five or so years needed for the main contract to be progressed. I was part of the Magic Carpet team.

The man who had negotiated the deal – a shadowy character who apparently lived in the Channel Islands – must have been a genius. Regretfully, the stresses and strains of negotiation took their toll on his health and he did not live long enough to enjoy his million-buck bonus.

Our flying routines were generally humdrum, sometimes boring holes (very boring ones) in the sky just to maintain flying currency. From time to time, though, we practised four-ship formation displays for special occasions. One time, our four-ship flew to the country's summer capital city – Jeddah on the west coast of Saudi Arabia, adjacent to the Red Sea; the wintertime capital was Riyadh. At Jeddah airfield I was astonished by the sight of one of the Saudis' previous air forces. Old de Havilland Vampire 5 aircraft, with flat tyres and perspex canopies yellowed by the twin effects of scorching sun and high humidity, were jammed together like discarded kids' toys. The Saudis' oil wealth seemed to encourage a *nouveau riche* attitude of disdain towards anything secondhand.

Lightning Mk 52.

Whether a car, an air conditioning unit or an aircraft, if an item broke down, it would be abandoned without a thought and a new one bought.

In mid-October 1966 we commenced rehearsals for a particular four-ship air display. The display, we had been briefed, should begin with the Lightnings performing reheat rotation take-offs in a five-second stream. On start-up for the second rehearsal, one of the Lightnings became unserviceable. As I was the most experienced Lightning pilot, I decided to offer my aircraft to one of the others, Piet Hay – a Rhodesian national who had flown as a member of the Red Arrows aerobatic team. Piet was an excellent pilot but had little experience on the Lightning. I therefore made my way to the air traffic control tower where I would observe the display and make notes for a subsequent debrief.

The first two Lightnings completed their take-offs and reheat rotations without problems. However, the third Lightning, flown by Piet Hay, experienced difficulties just at the point that he pulled back the stick for his reheat rotation. I could see at once that something was not right. The aircraft staggered up to a height of two hundred or so feet then appeared to stop dead in midair. It was as if some giant, invisible hand had reached out to grab the machine by its tailplane. The Lightning flicked onto its side, then the nose dropped before levelling at a position roughly in line with the horizon. Now the machine started to yaw slowly to the right; at any moment an earthwards plummet was inevitable. My heart leapt up to my mouth; I felt a cold shiver down my spine. I grabbed the nearest microphone and yelled: "*eject...Piet...eject.*" I learnt later that my words were wasted as the microphone was not connected to anything.

Piet, though, had not needed any words of encouragement. I held my breath as I witnessed his ejection. The cockpit canopy flew off, followed by the Martin Baker seat which, like a bullet, shot Piet away from his doomed Lightning. Within fractions of a second the drogue parachute deployed before the main parachute canopy billowed open, a last-ditch lifesaver that deposited Piet back onto mother earth. Unlike the tragic case of Capitaine Joel Dancel, Piet Hay had cheated death by a mere matter of seconds. I could breathe again; this time the chill finger of fate had been on our side.

The Lightning hit the ground just before its pilot, and not far away. I had a further moment of horror when Piet's parachute appeared to drift towards the fireball and towering plume of black smoke, but I need not have been concerned: he landed safely a few yards from the crash crater.

The Saudis, naturally enough, were anxious to know why one of their shiny new jets had crashed. Enter, stage left, one Roland Prosper 'Bee' Beamont CBE, DSO and bar, DFC and bar, Croix de guerre (Belgium – awarded posthumously in 2002), retired wing commander, fighter ace shot down in 1944 and made a prisoner-of-war after his 492nd operational mission, chief test pilot at the British Aircraft Corporation, chief test pilot of the P1/Lightning test programme, Lightning ace *extraordinaire* and all-round good egg. The two of us got on well.

"What technique have you been using for the reheat rotations?" he asked me.

I described how, as the Lightning reached an airspeed of 240 knots after take-off, the pilot would bring the stick back sharply then ease it forward again as the aircraft achieved a nose-up attitude of about 25 degrees. The resultant climb angle felt vertical to the pilot, and looked as such from the ground. The technique, taught to me from square one, had been approved by Fighter Command and was used throughout the Lightning force.

"Hmmm," said the great man. "That's what I'd heard."

"Is something wrong?"

"How much 'g' do you reckon to pull in the manoeuvre?"

"Four 'g', roughly."

"There's the problem then, right there," he said. I began to feel worried. "At what airspeed will the aircraft stall," he went on, "with 4 'g' applied?"

I glanced skywards as my mind performed mental gyrations: an aircraft's stall speed increased as the square root of the 'g' loading, therefore with 4 'g' applied the figure would double from around 120 knots to....

"240 knots," I said eventually. The great man said nothing. He just looked at me.

I exhaled a long, slow breath. "Oooh...shit," I said.

"Quite," he replied. "When I perform the manoeuvre, I apply only one to one-and-a-half 'g'. The 4 'g' pulled during your snatch technique is asking for trouble."

"But it's been done that way for years."

"Then you've all been very lucky."

RAF hunts for Russian Bears

A LONG-RANGE Russian "Bear" reconnaissance aircraft being "tailed" off Scotland by a Lightning of RAF Strike Command accompanied by a Victor refuelling tanker.

Russian aircraft are taking part in the large-scale Russian naval manoeuvres centred about 100 miles north of Scotland, and while low-flying Shackletons are shadowing the ships, the Lightnings are intercepting the planes—and then flying in company with them.

Strike Command pilots are becoming adept at "Bear hunting" and although unable to communicate with the Russian air-crews "appropriate hand signals are invariably exchanged."

Top: A 23 Squadron F6 in company with a Soviet Bear.

Above left: Daily Telegraph – 25 April 1970.

Above right: XR761 (AC) of 5 Squadron.

Left: Two 56(F) Squadron F6s with a Victor tanker.

Top left: A dramatic picture of F1A, XM214 at high speed.

Top right: XS920, an F6 of 11 Squadron armed with Firestreak infrared air-to-air missiles.

Above: 23 Squadron F3, XP 756, in a colour scheme of the mid-1960s.

Left: The prototype T Mk 5, XM967 approaching Filton aerodrome, Bristol.

Top: Seven F6s of 74 Squadron on the break.

Middle: Operational turn-around including Firestreak missile change on a 56(F) Squadron F3 at Akrotiri.

Bottom left: 14 Lightnings of 19(F) Squadron fly in formation to form a number '19'.

Bottom right: 19 Squadron F2As in vic formation.

Left: The Mk 53 multi-role export Lightning with wing and fuselage rocket pods.

Below: Two pilots sprint to their 56(F) Squadron aircraft in Akrotiri.

Before the great man left Saudi Arabia he thanked me for my co-operation and asked if I'd like a job with him as a production test pilot. I felt seriously flattered. However, some months later, when I rang the telephone number he had given me, he was out of the office. I explained to the fellow who answered the phone that I was interested in a test pilot job and that his boss had asked me to call. "Oh, he's always doing this," came the reply. "I'm afraid there are no vacancies."

Not long after this incident we got word that some RAF cadets visiting Saudi from the RAF College, Cranwell were in difficulty. The cadets, on an initiative exercise in the country, had run out of time, not to say initiative. Two Mini Mokes had been abandoned, one of which needed to be driven from Khamis Mushaif in the south-west of Saudi Arabia to Riyadh. What, I was asked, would I feel about taking on this 690-or-so-mile drive? "Sod it," I thought, "it'll be something different. I can pretend to be Lawrence of Arabia. Why not?"

The open-top, beach-buggy-style Mini Moke was, to put it politely, a spartan vehicle. I took with me just about every single item of clothing I owned and, as I set off, followed the line of what nowadays is an impressive motorway. Back then, though, the road was mostly sand and gravel and I progressed at what seemed like a snail's pace. By about six pm, when the December sun went down, I began to feel bitterly cold despite donning all of my clothing. I cursed for a fool the clown that had dreamed up this idea – which, of course, was me, so that didn't exactly help. I had three punctures en route but with only two spare wheels I needed to stop for puncture repair. Surprisingly, the motorway service stations had been built before the motorway itself and were open for business. At around three in the morning I pulled into one of these establishments. An elderly man came out of the building and stared at me suspiciously. His thin frame, dressed in grubby-looking robes, and his lank look made an unpromising initial impression. Looks, though, could be deceptive and before long, as the two of us communicated by a mixture of hand signals and soldiers' Arabic, we had become firm friends.

"Hummla, hummla wahid taman," he said (or words to that effect), and tugged at my sleeve. He led me round to an area at the back of the office where he pointed to a breeze-block structure with a sandy floor. In the centre of the floor lay the remains of a dying fire. My new friend crouched down on the dirt, blew strenuously into the embers and soon a roaring fire began to erupt. He placed a coffee pot on the fire, then left me to sip at a mug of coffee while he attended to the car. When he returned, I paid him and we chatted for a bit longer while I continued to thaw out. At length we shook hands and I was on my way in the Mini Moke again, mightily impressed by Bedouin hospitality.

By now my time in Saudi Arabia and my association with Lightnings was nearly over. By January, 1967 I had flown what I had assumed was my last Lightning flight. However, I had just returned to the UK and had been greeted in lovely green England by my lovely wife when Airwork contacted me. "We've got a problem," they said.

"Join the club," I said.

"King Hussein of Jordan is making a state visit to Saudi Arabia and they want a flypast."

"So?"

"The thing is…" a short cough and a long pause ensued. "Well, as you know, the flypast will involve four Lightnings but we have only three pilots."

"You cannot be serious?"

"I'm afraid it is serious."

I went back, more or less by return of post, so to speak, on the understanding that I would be involved in that one mission and that one mission alone. Oh, and that I would receive a further tax-free bounty of £500 (a small fortune in those days – enough to buy a decent car).

The occasion went well, the King of Jordan (a pilot himself) was evidently impressed. When, for the second time, I was greeted in lovely green England by my lovely wife at Heathrow airport, I knew that this time it really was the end. A flood of different emotions ran through my head as my wife ran up to me. I was about to embark on a whole new way of life and now, over forty-five years later, when I look back fondly on a long association with Qantas (I retired from the airline at the age of sixty, then spent four years with Cathay Pacific as a simulator instructor), I recall with nostalgia the many events which followed our move to Australia. My two sons both became pilots, my daughter became a nurse, my wife and I separated. In the study at my home in the Southern Highlands of New South Wales I am surrounded by models and photographs from air force days. It does not take much for my mind to drift back to Lightning experiences and to the events of 1966 in particular – such a seminal year in my life – and my eyes begin to mist over with memories as I breathe a small sigh of wistfulness.

CHAPTER 4

A DAY'S DIFFERENCE

ALAN WINKLES ON A DAY TRIP TO DIEPPE

The American controller's heavy southern drawl was hardly helpful. Perhaps the fellow had been unnerved by our predicament, maybe he was just having a bad day, I was unsure. Of one thing I was sure, however – that we had one last, crucial chance to land from this approach after which, if we failed to spot the fog-shrouded runway, we'd be forced to adopt the option of last resort: use of our Martin Baker ejection seats, a 'Martin Baker let-down' in popular parlance. The controller's hesitant and apparently conflicting instructions persisted and, like a couple of drunken men, our two Lightnings weaved their way left and right of the runway centre-line, up and down the approach glide-slope, as we pilots struggled to follow his directions.

The earlier decisions that had led us into this dire situation had been complex. Four Lightnings from 5(F) Squadron, having been selected from a cast of thousands (well, a handful anyway) to represent the Royal Air Force in a multinational flypast, would join forces with the likes of Mirages and F104 Starfighters to fly above an important military review near the French town of Dieppe. The chosen date, 19th August, 1967, would mark the twenty-fifth anniversary of an Allied amphibious strike in World War 2. That amphibious assault, an unmitigated disaster following flawed intelligence, poor planning by Lord Mountbatten and his staff, and inadequate support (to name but a few of the factors), had been met by robust enemy action. Of just over 6,000 Allied troops involved, most of whom were Canadian, more than 4,000 had been killed, wounded or captured. Some Canadian assault battalions had lost over 90% of their personnel. A quarter of a century on, the President of France, General Charles de Gaulle himself, would take the salute at the military review that would mark the Dieppe disaster of 1942.

However, the leader of our 5 Squadron four-ship, the squadron's commanding officer Wing Commander Winship, faced dilemmas. The occasion was momentous, we were intensely keen to do our bit – to 'show the flag' – but the current grim weather across the area, not to mention an equally foul forecast and unreliable diversion airfields, made the decision more than a little onerous. Another disaster twenty-five years after the original one would have been tough indeed. One reasonable bright spot, though, was the weather on the other side of the Channel which, over Dieppe itself, was workable if not altogether marvellous.

The four Lightnings, having flown from their 5 Squadron base at Binbrook in Lincolnshire to RAF Wattisham in Suffolk in order to be nearer Dieppe, were fully refuelled and ready to proceed. However, even though we pilots were poised, anxious to get going, we had to show patience as we remained in a crew room while our leader consulted by phone with headquarters. A needle of irritation went through my mind as we waited. I was 22 years of age, I had been on the squadron for less than a year. I had been selected to fly as number four in the formation; an honour and an important occasion for me personally as well as in a broader sense. To be thwarted by bad weather at the last minute would have been almost unbearable, especially when I contemplated my background that had led up to this moment.

Ten years had elapsed since my desire to become a fighter pilot was sparked when, as a schoolboy at Torquay Boys' Grammar School and as a member of the Air Training Corps, I had witnessed the 22-member Black Arrows formation team perform a loop in their Hunter aircraft. The spectacle had been breathtaking; I'd felt quite overwhelmed. As someone from a non-air force background (my father and grandfather had served in the army), the sight had somehow been all the more inspirational. When I'd watched that day, and while the Black Arrow team members had rehearsed over Torbay in preparation for the Exeter Air Show, I had known that the moment was a key one for me. Thoughts of hero-worship had undoubtedly beat fast in my young, twelve-year-old heart.

Five years later I was fortunate to be awarded a flying scholarship at the end of which I gained a civilian private pilots' licence. Perhaps even more fortunately, I was selected subsequently for the RAF's direct entry system. I could barely believe my luck, especially when the intensive flying training process went without holdups and my progress proved sufficiently good for me to be streamed onto fighters. It was just one week after my twenty-first birthday that I commenced work at the Lightning Operational Conversion Unit at RAF Coltishall, Norfolk.

"He's trying to nullify you...steal your thunder," I heard someone cry. I glanced back at the sound of raised voices at the far end of the crew room.

"I doubt it," came the reply. "He's the type that says the 'F' word loudly in meetings." The guffaws that followed this comment made me smile, though I soon reminded myself that, right now, there was little to smile about. I looked out of a window and stared at the murky scene beyond. A dimly lit sky, almost invisible at times, was closeted behind banks of low cloud and mist that swirled across the airfield. Occasional improvements in visibility would raise my spirits until, as if immersed into a great bath of grey cotton wool, parts of the airfield would become enshrouded again.

Suddenly I looked across the crew room as Wing Commander Winship returned. His expression was pensive, his eyes pained and distant-looking as he re-joined us. "Okay, chaps," he said, speaking slowly while he glanced at each of us in turn. "I've talked things through with HQ Fighter Command and..." he hesitated "although conditions are pretty borderline, I've decided that we should give it a shot. We've been given a green light from HQ." He went on to explain that 'amber' meteorological conditions were anticipated at nearby airfields which could be used if Wattisham was declared 'red'. Red conditions were below our operating minima and therefore not acceptable, but the prognosis, he said, even though less than ideal, was sufficiently good for us to proceed, especially in view of the flight's importance.

After a brief re-cap of salient points, the four of us walked out to our aircraft. Groundcrews, some with facial expressions of doubt when they glanced skywards, assisted while we strapped in to individual cockpits. At a signal from the leader, all four Lightnings then commenced engine-start procedures. Before long, when cleared by air traffic control, we began to taxy towards the runway. At the take-off point, the first two Lightnings moved ahead while number three, flown by Major Bill Beardsley (United States Air Force), and myself as number four held back briefly. We watched the first pair take off in an impressive whirl of reheat flame and local mist before we moved on to the runway for our own pairs' take-off procedure. At the nod of Major Beardsley's head, I released my brakes. At a further nod I pushed both of my engine throttles outboard and fully forward to engage maximum reheat. A sudden punch in the back confirmed that my reheats had lit and now, while I followed my leader's every move as we accelerated along the runway, my peripheral vision picked up alternate shadows of black and white from adjacent mist banks.

Soon, when both pairs of Lightnings had joined up, the four-ship turned due south to head for Dieppe. The transit flight did not take long and as we approached the rendezvous point a quick glance at the time confirmed that we were exactly on schedule. Others in the larger formation, however, were evidently less diligent time-keepers. With no signs of the expected Mirages and F104 Starfighters, our four Lightnings had to set up an orbital pattern at 2,000 feet while we waited. Meantime, minds began to work feverishly as meagre fuel margins started steadily to diminish. Eventually, twelve minutes late, the other aircraft finally turned up after which, still worried about our Lightnings' low fuel reserves, all aircraft types moved into their briefed positions for the grand flypast. Soon, with the 5 Squadron contingent in a neat box pattern, the entire formation set off to overfly the resplendent military parade.

I was probably too preoccupied to think of the great man below as he stood, lofty, imperious, at the saluting dais. Just last month, on a visit to Canada, De Gaulle had stirred up controversy in a speech when he had announced *Vive le Québec libre*! (long live free Quebec). "Canadians do not need to be liberated," an irate Lester B Pearson, the Canadian prime minister, had declared subsequently. De Gaulle had left Canada abruptly two days later without completing his schedule. Never again would he return to that country. 'There is not a scrap of generosity about this man,' Churchill had written about De Gaulle in a letter shortly before D-Day, 'who only wishes to pose as the saviour of France in this operation.' De Gaulle's punctilious standards, though, were admired by many and no doubt he received generous applause as we overflew when he took the salute that day.

On completion of the flypast, the sundry elements broke off as previously planned to make their own way back to various bases. Wing Commander Winship, having initiated a climb and instructed his Lightnings to move from box formation to finger four, ordered us to change radio frequency to 'Eastern Radar'. He checked us in on the new frequency then, after some difficulty establishing contact with the controller, asked for meteorological updates of airfields across East Anglia. It was at this point that I caught my breath and felt a knot of anxiety form in my stomach. As, one after the other, each airfield was declared state red, a poignant pause ensued. Because of the initial problems making contact with Eastern Radar, suitable continental diversions such as Volkel in Holland or Florennes in Belgium were now too distant.

After an ominous hesitation, the controller suddenly piped up: "Standby one...an update from Bentwaters is just coming through...standby." I could almost picture physical strands of suspense form in nearby cockpits as we waited. "Okay..." the controller spoke in a deliberate fashion as he went on: "Bentwaters has declared state amber. Do you wish to divert there?"

The wing commander's voice sounded mighty relieved as he confirmed that we would, indeed, head for Bentwaters – and ASAP to boot. Hastily, he issued new instructions: Major Beardsley and I would make a pairs approach to the airfield ahead of the wing commander himself and his number two, Flight Lieutenant Stuart Miller. (As number four in the formation, I had employed more throttle 'pumping' than the others and therefore had consumed more fuel.)

At an appropriate moment, when the four-ship had split into two pairs as briefed, I moved into an echelon starboard position while I held formation on Major Beardsley. As I did so, I cast a last, gloomy glance at my fuel gauges: 600 lbs on each side. I was already below the normal landing figure of 800 lbs per side. I knew that the major and I had been placed, as they say, firmly on the spot. We faced a crucial, one-off opportunity without the luxury of a second chance.

The initial descent from high altitude worked well until, at a range of around ten miles from Bentwaters and with our altitude settled at 1,500 feet, we were instructed to change to the talk-down controller's radio frequency. When we checked in with the new controller, at once it became obvious that this man, with his southern US drawl, was in a jittery state. We had the advantage that Major Beardsley, as a native American, could interpret the fellow's drawl better than some, however, in spite of this, when the controller's instructions became increasingly erratic we realised that our already-serious circumstances were about to become even more so. While we weaved our way randomly left and right of the runway centre-line, above and below the correct approach glide-path, I felt a further sense of icy apprehension in my stomach.

By now the visibility was down to near-zero. From my echelon starboard position I could just make out Major Beardsley's right wingtip but not a lot else: no fuselage, no tailplane – nothing. I stared as hard as I could, as if this might help to enhance my vision. It occurred to me, though, that if I stared too hard I might get caught up in a fierce, disorientating hallucination. I needed every ounce of concentration that I could muster. There was no question of breaking off; my position, frankly, was one of desperation. Despite, at times, having no more than a faint impression of wing metal to guide me, I knew that

I had little alternative but to hang in there. I felt a bitter loneliness as, isolated in my Lightning, I experienced the sensation of being drawn ever closer to the brink of calamity.

When we reached an altitude of 250 feet the controller announced: "You're at break-off height – talk-down ends."

"Keep talking!" yelled Major Beardsley. At this stage we were well left of the runway centre-line and unable to discern any runway lights.

Time appeared to distort while subsequent seconds ticked by. As if descending into a form of physical, chilling twilight zone, we continued down. I felt trapped – forced into activity that was contrary to training and instinct. Then, quite suddenly, to my right, my peripheral vision picked up a glimpse of lights. Powerful, pulsing, American-style runway approach lights became visible through the swirls of low cloud and mist. Against all normal procedures, I decided to break away from my leader and to turn immediately hard right. I headed towards strobe lights which, like some surreal, last-gasp lifesaver, seemed to beckon me towards the now-visible runway.

What happened next remains a blur in my memory. I have hazy recollections of a series of vigorous manoeuvres at very low altitude after which I was able to land. I announced briefly that I had done so. Meanwhile, I recall a sense of horror when I saw Major Beardsley's tailpipes disappear to my left as his Lightning climbed back up into the gloom. I remember thinking that he hadn't a hope in hell of achieving a successful landing now. I was wrong, though. He hauled his aircraft into a blind 360 degree turn at the end of which he managed to spot the runway strobe lights and land behind me. Just thirty seconds after that, Wing Commander Winship and his number two landed in turn.

Later, when I reflected on the incident, I would do so with a haunting sense of the unreal. Facial images would enter my head as if our formation members had suddenly appeared and started to swim out to sea without looking back. Meanwhile, as a drowning disaster seemed inevitable, observers hoped, prayed, wondered if fate's steely fist might loosen its grip. It was mere reverie, of course, but enough to make my conscious state realise that the experience at Dieppe that day was something I could never forget.

What a difference a day can make.

TO PEE OR NOT TO PEE, THAT IS THE QUESTION

It was some months after the Dieppe saga that I became involved in a long distance deployment flight direct from Binbrook to RAF Muharraq on Bahrain in the Persian Gulf. Supported by Victor air-to-air refuelling tankers, this was due be the longest non-stop flight undertaken by RAF fighters to date.

While technical aspects of the eight-hour flight did not worry us unduly, we were uneasy about some of the practical implications. For example, we would need to eat, drink and relieve ourselves. The Lightning's normal flight profiles did not involve any of these functions. We were conscious that the esteemed Lightning aircraft designers at the English Electric Company, when they had gazed at their technical drawings and as they had whizzed their slide rules this way and that, had failed to take into consideration one or two rather significant factors.

The eat and drink issues were resolved reasonably readily. It would be officially acceptable, so we were told, for suitably prepared liquids and bite-sized air force sandwiches to be popped into the mouth during brief removals of the oxygen mask. Fair enough, we thought, but what about the relieving-oneself aspect? Regretfully, the solution to this proved to be a little less straightforward.

Four Lightnings were involved in the deployment – two pairs of Lightnings, each pair separated by a fifteen-minute interval. I was allocated the number two position in the second pair. The hour was early when, on the twentieth day of May in 1968, we were scheduled to take off. Before we manned our cockpits, however, we had to prepare them for the forthcoming eight-hour marathon.

The cramped Lightning cockpit, less than ideal for in-flight catering artistry, nonetheless offered opportunities for the imaginatively minded. As I climbed my aircraft's cockpit access ladder that morning I clutched – in addition to maps, radio frequency books and other paraphernalia – a box of rations supplied by RAF Binbrook's catering section. The rations had to be distributed around diverse nooks and crannies within the cockpit's modest confines. Pressed up against the perspex canopy and wedged at a convenient angle, I placed my bite-sized cheese sandwiches.

In similar fashion on the opposite console, I secured two cardboard drink containers, an apple and a small pack of biscuits. Next, I carefully arranged two Aero chocolate bars within the radar's viewing shade, a fold-up rubber device. Lastly, I used one of my flying suit pockets to stow a specially designed so-called pee-bag, acquired for us from the United States Air Force.

Before long we were ready to depart. After engine start, and while I followed the lead Lightning to Binbrook's runway-in-use for take-off, I taxied as judiciously as possible. The Lightning's notorious, but necessarily ferocious, take-off technique caused one or two problems, though most of my in-flight meal remained intact – with one exception, however. By the time our formation was close to the River Thames and our first in-flight refuel had been completed, I decided to check my airborne radar. As soon as I unfolded the rubber viewing shade I spotted trouble. The inside of the shade itself, lined with a thin layer of melted chocolate, was a forlorn and sticky sight. At the end of the viewing shade the two-and-a-half inch radar screen was obscured by a covering of chocolate chaos. The problem had been caused, I assumed, by a combination of atmospheric pressure differential and heat generated by the radar's cathode ray tube. Despite an apposite name, the Aero bar with its inbuilt air bubbles had been an unfortunate choice by the Binbrook catering section. For most of our transit across France I used my fingers to scoop up a gooey, chocolatey mess – hoping, meanwhile, that the cheese sandwiches had not suffered some other form of in-flight modification.

Our route took the formation in the vicinity of Sicily's Mount Etna which, in full eruption, by chance gave us some remarkable images of nature's potency. Beyond Sicily we turned due east to fly above the Mediterranean Sea towards Crete and Cyprus. In order to avoid warring Middle East nations, we turned due north from Cyprus to overfly Turkey.

At length, when I saw Turkey's rugged landscape come into view, I knew that the *moment critique* had come: the challenge of my USAF pee-bag was nigh.

As a six-foot-two-tall individual, my only hope of success was to undo my seat straps before I attempted any contortionist's tricks. I was aware, too, that the restrictive design of my waterproof immersion suit would be unhelpful. Determined, nonetheless, to do my bit for the Binbrook doctor's experiment (he wanted urine samples to test for blood sugar levels), I ensured that the Lightning's autopilot system was engaged before I released the seat straps and the struggle got underway.

The proceedings proved to be more time-consuming than anticipated. One advantage, however, of having wriggled and wormed my way into the necessary position was that I achieved an improved panorama of Turkey's pastoral scenery below. With the apex of my bone dome pushed precariously against the Lightning's perspex canopy, and with my feet pressed hard against the rudder pedals, I managed to stretch out reasonably well. The peculiar posture, though, with my chin squashed into my neck and my eyes staring down at the chocolatey radar, seemed to make me feel quite light-headed. My thoughts began to spin around and around until I wanted to laugh out loud like some kid. How absurd I would look, I mused, if a passer-by should chance across me now...

"...clear to join port side..." the Victor tanker captain's voice suddenly interrupted my mental wanderings. As if at the flick of a switch, my brain re-engaged firmly with reality. Preoccupied with the doctor's experiment, I had failed to notice what every good fighter pilot should notice as a matter of course – details like fuel state, navigational position, nearest diversion airfield. By now I was low on fuel, I was unsure of my position, I wasn't even strapped in. Furthermore, I had entered an area of cirrus cloud and was no longer in visual contact with the Victor tanker or with the other Lightning.

With nervous speculation about an unfriendly interview with my boss, even a board of inquiry if matters turned seriously pear shaped, I hastily turned on my chocolate radar. The device would take two minutes to warm up – two minutes I could ill-afford to waste, even so it might prove useful, especially as by now I had scraped away sufficient chocolate to make the screen usable. Meanwhile, I tweaked the Lightning's autopilot five degrees right in the hope that a heading adjustment would help me to glimpse the Victor's contrail. Sure enough, this worked: through surrounding patchy cirrus I could spot the contrail. Without further ado I advanced the Lightning's throttles and before long, as I caught up with the Victor and the other Lightning, I reached them just as the latter's pilot was worriedly calling for me to confirm my position.

"Ready to refuel from the port hose," I said nonchalantly. In the subsequent debrief I did not admit what had happened.

With the in-flight refuelling completed, and as we approached Lake Van in the north-eastern reaches of Turkey, the formation experienced so-called 'meaconing'. This was an attempt by operators in Soviet territory, nowadays the Republic of Armenia, to lure us over to their side of the border by interference with navigational equipment. The efforts, however, were crass and futile apart from minor entertainment value from our standpoint. Beyond Lake Van we turned south into Iran, past Tehran and towards the oilfields of Abadan, at which stage Kuwait and the northern waters of the Persian Gulf started to appear on the horizon. After interminable tracts of desolate desert, the watery contrast was stark – blue-green and cold against the sky which had developed the glittering, hazy brilliance of full afternoon.

By now our marathon flight was nearly over. When we initiated descent to Bahrain I began to realise just how jaded I felt, nevertheless both Lightnings managed a fast, low run over the airfield at RAF Muharraq to make our presence known after which, as we landed and taxied to the dispersal area, and as I glimpsed the barren, sandy surrounds, I had a fine feeling of job satisfaction. The flight had offered exceptional experiences, even the opportunity to indulge the good doctor's experiment. Despite a look of distaste on the airman's face when I handed him the results, the experiment had proved a success.

Inevitable debriefs and paperwork followed and by the time we were driven away from the aircraft dispersal area to the officers' mess, dusk was evident. The period between night and day is brief in that part of the world, but I felt a warmness inside me and felt like humming a little tune as the vehicle sped ahead through the darkened desert stretches. Jaded or not, I knew that, in more ways than one, this had been one of life's 'eureka' days. What a difference, indeed, a day can make.

CHAPTER 5

PRODIGIOUS PLANS

Wing Commander Terry Adcock at his desk in Penang.

TERRY ADCOCK RECOLLECTS A TENSE INSPECTION

The plan seemed straightforward enough. At least, that was what we reckoned at the time. We even had a back-up plan – a Plan B, if you like. I have to admit, though, that we did not anticipate a Plan C, let alone a Plan D or E. As things turned out, this was unfortunate.

The pomp and ceremony that go with a Royal Air Force station's annual inspection by the air officer commanding will involve many time-consuming but obligatory, if irksome, preparations. Parade-ground drills must be rehearsed, office floors swept, surfaces polished, paintwork painted, windows wiped, stores stored, cookhouses scrubbed, and messes must be made to look unmessy. Personnel will be required to set-to as every conceivable nook and cranny across the station will be spruced-up ahead of the big day. Folk will be on edge; future postings and promotions can be influenced by an inspection's success or otherwise.

As the commanding officer of a training unit (3 Squadron) at the Lightning

Operational Conversion Unit at RAF Coltishall in Norfolk, I was, of course, deeply involved when the time came, in mid-May 1970, for that station's annual inspection. The wing commander in charge of the operations wing at the time had ambitious ideas. "We'll plan to scramble twenty-five aircraft plus one spare," he said at a briefing some days before the inspection. A few raised eyebrows, even the odd sharp intake of breath, were evident when he said this. "And I'm sure," he went on, "that the AOC will be duly impressed."

"Twenty-five, sir?" asked someone.

A montage of Terry Adcock's penultimate Lightning flight in Cyprus.

"Yes, twenty-five." The wing commander hesitated as he looked around the room. Nobody spoke but facial expressions revealed thoughts that varied from 'good gracious,' to 'shit', to 'you'll be lucky, old son'. Despite such looks of discouragement, the wing commander persisted with his briefing while he explained that his planned flypast of twenty-five Lightnings would entail neat box formations for the benefit of the air vice-marshal. In the event of bad weather, however, the twenty-five aircraft would take off in a stream, one after the other, then climb up to altitude before returning to Coltishall individually in a pre-planned sequence.

Questions followed the wing commander's briefing until eventually, when the meeting broke up, most of us were reasonably happy with the plan. It was not until some days later, on the morning of the inspection date itself, that doubts returned. "We're expecting a cold front to pass overhead Coltishall this afternoon," said the weatherman. He spoke in fine, confident tones and I speculated on whether he possessed plenary meteorological powers. I glanced out of an adjacent window. The sky was overcast and looked threatening, but the local visibility was okay, there were no signs of rain yet and the surface wind coincided, more or less, with the runway direction.

"Exactly when do you expect the front to pass overhead?" someone asked. The weatherman hummed and harred at this. Clearly there were ambiguities and dark places in the meteorological mastery. "So much for the plenary powers," I thought. In spite of this, the wing commander announced that we would proceed with Plan A – the neat box-formation option. He reckoned that the flypast would be completed and all the aircraft safely back on the ground before the cold front went through. In view of the uncertain timing I expressed reservations, but I had to agree with the wing commander's point that we were a very experienced group of Lightning pilots and that, furthermore, as a training unit we possessed a large number of two-seaters. About 40 Lightning pilots in total would be flying in the formation. "If ever there was a formation that could cope with a bit of bad weather," said the wing commander, "this is surely it."

At this, we dispersed in anticipation of the air vice-marshal's arrival. As the appointed hour approached, the parade formed up, drill sergeants bellowed orders, tidy lines of airmen and airwomen stood shoulder-to-shoulder. All stood rigidly to attention when the air vice-marshal was driven up in a highly-polished car from which he stepped out to inspect the rows of personnel before he made for a saluting dais. Soon, the band struck up the Royal Air Force March and the parade began to move past the dais. The 'eyes right' order was given; the marchers obeyed in an instant; the air vice-marshal saluted severely. Meanwhile, families and friends, wives in posh frocks, miscellaneous folk, had assembled near the dais so as to admire the proceedings.

Before long, when the parade had been declared an official success, participants were dismissed to make their way to places of work. In my own case, this was the 3 Squadron hangar where I had to wait around until the air vice-marshal had concluded his inspection of the wing operations set-up. I knew that organisation well; I had been the squadron leader in charge until my recent change to a flying job and I was anxious, therefore, that the inspection there should go well.

In a reflective mood while I waited, I recalled a particular incident that had occurred shortly before my posting. The wing operations room, solely a communications centre in peacetime, became the airfield's command and control centre in the event of war. As part of this war role, the room's walls were covered in acres of maps, some of which displayed areas as far away as eastern Europe. One night, during a markedly dull communications exercise, I saw that the officer on duty, Flight Lieutenant Benny Baranowski (he was born in Poland), was staring wistfully at the eastern European section of the map. He was normally an ebullient, upbeat character, so I asked him why he looked despondent. There was little to do, he said with a sigh, but to stare at the map and to think bad thoughts.

"Bad thoughts?" I said.

"Yes, sir," he said.

"What happened, Benny?"

"Can't remember. No point to remember. Too much in the past."

There was a long silence.

"We cannot help who we are," I said.

"Hmmm. Some things hard to discuss. Besides..."

"What?"

"Not so nice there."

"What's not so nice?"

"Everything. Crap cars, crap cookers, crap everything." He looked cross. Clearly, though, materialism was not the point. The issues that bothered him ran deeper.

"Go on," I said.

He glanced at me. Such talk was unusual, whether in the work environment or in the mess, but there was scarcely any current activity, the room was quiet, few personnel were on duty and we could not be overheard. He looked around the room before, in low tones, his story came tumbling out. As his commanding officer I knew a little of his background, but that night, while I listened to some of his detailed descriptions, I became at once saddened and enthralled.

He talked of how, in the early part of World War 2 when he was a nineteen-year-old lad, all of his family had been killed – murdered, in all probability – and he had ended up in a concentration camp. He had managed to escape and, despite suffering from pneumonia, he had commenced a mammoth walk which had finished up in southern Europe. By fair means or foul, he had made his way from there to the United Kingdom where he had applied to join the Royal Air Force. To his very considerable credit, especially in view of the circumstances, he had become a commissioned officer.

When he had ended his account, and with a sense of emotion, I stood up and walked to the section of map that portrayed Poland. He joined me and together we removed the perspex cover in order to cut away the offending area.

It was some time later, in unexpected circumstances, that this small kindness was repaid.

Flight Lieutenant Baranowski was a large man – a champion shot-putter and discus thrower – who possessed uncommonly large hands. After a dining-in night at the officers' mess one evening, I became embroiled in a nefarious game of mess rugby. At the bottom of the scrum and with bodies piled high above me, I struggled to find breath. Then a curious thing happened. The load began mysteriously to lighten and before long I found myself placed on a stool as a welcome glass of beer was thrust in my direction. Flight Lieutenant Baranowski's massive hands had removed individuals one by one from the scrum, hurled them into far corners of the room, then lifted me off the floor. In pretty short shrift, the scrum had been ruthlessly terminated. Benny had returned a favour and no-one argued with Benny.

My nerves suddenly stiffened when I caught sight of the highly-polished car as the vehicle headed in my direction. Anxiously, I checked that my best air force hat was straight and I stood to attention. The vehicle swept up in a suitably dignified manner. I saluted and moved forward to help the air vice-marshal from his car. "Hello, Squadron Leader Adcock," he said, "hope I haven't kept you waiting."

"Not at all, sir," I said obsequiously and less than truthfully, "the 3 Squadron pilots have been assembled in the crew room."

Handshakes and polite conversations in the crew room ensued while the pilots, all dressed in clean flying suits, chatted with the air vice-marshal. Before long, however, conversations had to be curtailed as the time for the planned flypast drew near. By now late morning, the pilots gathered up their flying kit and soon, as the unusual and impressive number of Lightning pilots began to walk to their allotted aircraft, activities were observed by the attendant wives, families and friends. The air vice-marshal himself was driven to the air traffic control tower from where he would watch events.

With one exception (a Lightning that suffered a starter fire and consequently had to be abandoned) the start-up went well. A remarkable spectacle followed as the remaining twenty-four machines (plus one spare) taxied towards the take-off point. As my section of four Lightning T5s brought up the rear, I had a grandstand view. With a sense of awe, I watched the aircraft line up in turn for take-off in pairs. Throttles were advanced before brake release; a heat haze began to shimmer above the runway – a mirage-like effect that spread gradually to a wider area; the collective potency produced by so many Rolls-Royce Avon engines was a sight to behold.

When my turn came, I experienced some turbulence during the take-off run but not enough to worry me unduly. What did concern me, though, was the sight of aircraft ahead – or rather the lack of such sight. As the machines disappeared swiftly into cloud it was evident that the frontal system had started to approach sooner than forecast.

My mind now went into overdrive. With recovery problems to the airfield looming, I could not see the point of a climb to high altitude. I decided, therefore, to remain below cloud. I led my section of four aircraft out to sea towards an area of improved cloudbase. On the aircraft radio I instructed the pilots in my formation to use their airborne radars to lock-on to the other Lightnings ahead and to keep me informed of the situation. It soon became obvious, though, that problems had developed at altitude as the other formations struggled to establish their relative positions. Just as mind-boggling levels of confusion began to take hold, the order was given for all aircraft to initiate recovery to Coltishall without delay.

I now reckoned that my best option would be to sneak back to Coltishall ahead of the masses returning from high altitude – the 20 other Lightnings, plus the spare, plus a random Chipmunk aircraft that had inconveniently and tiresomely entered the toxic mix. I turned at once towards the airfield and increased airspeed as I led my formation back for a visual break and landing. The weather at this stage, although hardly wonderful, was still sufficiently good to permit visual approaches.

At a range of some seven miles from the airfield I suddenly caught sight of another formation of four Lightnings: the wing commander operations and his team had arrived just ahead. As I watched his formation break into the circuit, I manoeuvred to arrange appropriate separation. At the point of breaking into the circuit, however, we heard the controller's anguished voice call: "*overshoot for crash diversion*". The wing commander's Lightning had careered into the runway crash barrier; the three others in his formation had been instructed to fly to a diversion airfield.

Meanwhile, as the air vice-marshal in the air traffic control tower took in the developing drama, he quietly (and prudently) announced his departure from the scene ("things seems to be getting a bit busy," he told the duty pilot, "perhaps I should leave you to it.") The ambitious plans to impress our important visitor had begun to turn distinctly, hideously, pear shaped.

When I called "downwind for precautionary landing" (a term used in the Lightning force to indicate that, in the event of tail parachute failure, the aircraft would not overshoot as should be the case ordinarily) the controller replied: "there's an aircraft in the crash barrier, divert immediately."

"Negative," I said, "I'm short of fuel."

"Understood," said the controller after a pause, "in that case you're clear to

An instance of crash barrier engagement (92 Squadron).

land precautionary."

As I had over-ridden the controller I knew my approach and landing had to be right. My finals turn, though, proved to be more than a little eye-watering; suddenly I found that I was struggling to line up with the runway. "Confirm the surface wind?" I asked the controller tersely. His reply sent a shudder of apprehension down my spine. With the frontal zone's passage the wind had veered through almost 180 degrees. We were, in effect, using the wrong runway. No wonder there were problems with the finals turn. And no wonder, I thought, an aircraft has ended up in the barrier. At once I overshot for a second attempt. This time, with proper allowance for the new wind, I managed a successful landing behind the others in my formation who, having observed my first approach, had duly altered their own approach paths.

Any sense of relief, however, was short-lived. As I taxied back to dispersal I became aware of mounting ordeals for the formations still airborne. The weather states at nominated diversion airfields had started to deteriorate and moreover, to add to the unfolding chaos, one of the Lightnings had developed radio problems. All air traffic on the same frequency had to endure a continuous, aggravating stream of radio checks mixed with puffs and blows as the pilot tried to establish contact. My heart sank: vivid images raced through my mind of a calamitous affair some years ago at Leconfield under eerily similar circumstances. On that occasion, the outcome had been the loss of a number of valuable Hawker Hunter aircraft when the pilots had been forced to eject from their machines.

Suddenly, while I taxied back towards the dispersal area, I caught a glimpse of a Lightning as the machine made a low approach above the still-occupied crash barrier. The pilot, by now doubtless very low on fuel and very devoid of ideas, appeared determined to land his aircraft into the wind. Ignoring all standard rules and procedures he flew low above the crash barrier before he manoeuvred vigorously to land his aeroplane. I felt as if I was watching some kind of live horror movie. Instinctively, I held my breath as the Lightning hurtled down an inadequate length of runway. Luckily the tail parachute deployed correctly and the pilot was able to bring his aircraft to a halt just in time. This was the last aircraft to land at Coltishall that day. I let out a long, low, whistle of astonishment, shook my head with a sense of woe and clambered hastily from my cockpit.

At length, when the limited number of pilots that had made it back to Coltishall met up in their crew room, nervous chatter accompanied graphic accounts of individual experiences. However, when we learnt that, unlike at Leconfield, all of our aircraft had landed safely, the air of relief was palpable. This did not, though, impede ongoing, if somewhat embellished, recollections of a Plan B – if not a Plan C, D or E – that would long remain in the collective memories of those involved.

FINE FINALE

Self-sufficiency, so we are told, is a good thing. It was some dozen years later when I had to put this to the test in no uncertain terms. By then I had been promoted to the rank of wing commander and, as the commanding officer of 5(F) Squadron based at RAF Binbrook in Lincolnshire, I faced a Plan B of an altogether different kind. The circumstances were as unexpected as they were unusual.

Initial plans to base Lightnings on the Ascension Islands to secure the route south during the 1982 Falklands campaign were rapidly abandoned when someone realised that the runway and other surfaces at Ascension airfield were unsuitable. With the airfield's relatively low LCN (load classification number) the Lightning's skinny, high pressure tyres would have caused the aircraft wheels to sink axle-deep into Ascension tarmac.

As a Plan B, therefore, Headquarters 11 Group declared that our Lightnings should undertake a detachment to Cyprus where we would practise weapon firing – an armament practice camp or APC. In more normal times we would in-flight refuel to Cyprus in one hop. However, as the Victor in-flight refuelling aircraft were heavily committed to the Falklands campaign, on this occasion we would have to make alternative arrangements. This meant that ten Light-

Flying across the Alps en route to Cyprus.

nings in two sections of five would be required to fly along airways, stick to air traffic control routes and procedures, and generally act like airliners (minus, regretfully, the airline hostesses). Five separate legs were planned with four stops – Dijon in France, Pisa and Brindisi in Italy, and Souda Bay in Crete. At Pisa and Souda Bay we would rest overnight.

It was at the first stop that I began to appreciate the magnitude of our undertaking. In addition to navigational planning, submission of flight plans and other aircrew-type duties, the pilots had to refuel the aircraft, fit pre-positioned tail parachutes, top-up starter systems and carry out other essential engineering turn-round procedures. By the time I climbed back into my cockpit for the next leg I felt hot and hassled, my hands smelt of aviation fuel, and a hundred-and-one details persisted to spin around in my head. I vowed never again to take for granted the sterling work performed by our engineering turn-round crews.

Fortunately, groundcrews had been flown in ahead for the overnight stops at Pisa and at Souda Bay. Our departure from Souda Bay for the final leg on 10th June 1982 worked well until, as we took up a heading for Akrotiri in Cyprus, the controller instructed us to hold at 6,000 feet to the west of Crete. I knew at once that this was a non-starter: the Lightnings' fuel margins were typically tight and any delay would have meant a return to Souda Bay to refuel before a second attempt.

"Your transmissions are intermittent," I said to the controller who promptly repeated his instruction for us to hold at 6,000 feet to the west.

"You're still intermittent," I said, "we're climbing as per the flight plan and will keep well clear of incoming traffic." An irate-sounding controller immediately repeated his instructions.

"Your message," I said, "is not understood, but thank you for your assistance. Have a good day." At this, I ordered the formation to change to a different radio frequency, but not before we had picked up the controller's rant as he expressed choice, if not altogether polite, remarks.

We continued due east for Cyprus and as I glanced down at the blue-green translucence of the Mediterranean Sea, I could not avoid a sense of wistfulness. After more than two years on 5 Squadron, I realised that I could expect a posting quite soon. My Lightning days were well and truly numbered, and I knew it. As I thought about the long period of time I had spent within the Lightning world, disconnected memories of events large and small seemed to come flooding back. I recalled, for instance, a bizarre occasion when I was despatched from Coltishall to the Ministry of Defence to agree a squadron number; a new reserve squadron was about to be formed and the powers-that-be at Coltishall were keen on the designation 'Number 65 Squadron'.

My experience at the Ministry of Defence could have come straight from the television programme 'Yes, Minister'. I was hustled into an obscure office where the desk officer produced a small box of cards which he placed on his desktop. Available squadron numbers were written on individual cards with a separate card for each squadron. I explained that 65 Squadron would do us nicely, thank you, as this squadron had a fighter background, was the favoured choice back at Coltishall, and we knew that it was available. "No chance," said the desk officer, "these squadron numbers must remain in sequence and the next one has a background in maritime operations."

"But..." my discomfiture must have been clear.

"Would you like a cup of coffee?" the desk officer asked pleasantly.

"Thank you," I said, "I would."

"Then kindly excuse me for a minute or two while I deal with the makings." He winked and as soon as he had disappeared from the office I grabbed the small box, fished around for the card marked 'Number 65 Squadron' and placed it on top of the pile.

"Now where were we?" the desk officer asked amiably as he returned carrying our cups of coffee. I said nothing but I looked at him, glanced at the

Formation flying over Cyprus.

small box, then looked back at him again. "Ah, yes. About the squadron number," he went on. "Well, as I say, my hands are tied, I'm afraid, and we'll have to stick to the order in this box. Now let me see…" he picked up the top card. "Well, well," he said, "now there's a thing. It looks like I'm going to have to allocate you Number 65 Squadron."

Suddenly I spotted a distinctive pattern on my radar screen. The island of Cyprus was in our sights. As the formation initiated descent towards Akrotiri, my thoughts seemed in turmoil. While disjointed images about the end of my flying days persisted in my mind, I mused about how my present way of life would swiftly, sadly become a far-off and flimsy memory. The giant leap from cockpit to desk would mean an inevitable metamorphosis; like that desk officer in the Ministry of Defence, maybe I was destined to become a mere ministry man. As if alerted to a looming precipice with treacherous waters below, I felt a mood of growing gloominess.

The distractions of Cyprus, however, and the business of our armament practice camp provided good antidotes to 'bad thoughts'. Along with all of our squadron personnel, my mind seemed preoccupied, too, with distant events in the Falklands. Four days after the squadron reached Cyprus a ceasefire was declared but the ramifications lingered on. I recalled the reaction of our squadron pilots all those weeks ago when told of plans to send us to Ascension: half seemed eager and excited, the other half went rather quiet. A peacetime air force could seem decidedly different to one embroiled in war.

Terry Adcock in a Lightning cockpit.

It was towards the end of the detachment in Cyprus, perhaps when I was off-guard and maybe even in the process of self-rebuke for unnecessary 'bad thoughts', that the bombshell struck. It came in the form of a buff-coloured envelope. When handed to me, I gazed at the innocuous yet life-changing item, turned it over a few times then ripped it open. I was, indeed, destined to become a ministry man.

Plans now had to be put into effect in a manner, as the saying goes, both fast and furious. A number of issues, while not exactly pernicious, nonetheless seemed to grow daily in complexity. For one thing, I was given just two weeks for my family to vacate our ex-officio house and move to a different married quarter. In twenty-four years of marriage, this would become home number twenty-five. I decided that, in view of the hectic arrangements required on return to Binbrook, my last flying on the squadron should be in Cyprus. I decided, too, that my final day of flying should involve all fifteen of the squadron pilots in Cyprus: a formation of nine Lightnings (with one spare acting as whipper-in) followed by a formation of five.

We flew over Akrotiri Bay towards the local hospital where, with prior agreement, we roared past at balcony level for the benefit of staff and patients. We then overflew individual service units as a farewell thank you. I noted how personnel rushed outside to watch and how their vigorous hand waves demonstrated appreciation.

Eleven Lightnings of 5(F) Squadron fly in formation to form a number '5' over Akrotiri.

At the conclusion of the second formation, we repaired to the officers' mess for a special luncheon after which, at an opportune moment, I walked alone to the bottom of the mess garden where I wept in private. The proceedings seemed surreal and it was not until later that evening, when I stared up at the frozen stars in the Cypriot night sky and watched a cloud drift across the face of the moon, that reality suddenly struck. I had a curious feeling of detachment. I somehow knew that I would never pilot an aircraft again and, indeed, I never have done.

CHAPTER 6

I SAY, I SAY!

Flight Lieutenant Terry Davies by a 29(F) Squadron Lightning in Cyprus, October 1968.

TERRY DAVIES ADMITS TO NOT-SO-PETTY LARCENY

The distant bark of dogs, the wauling of cats, a child's wail all conspired to add to my already-heightened sense of tension. I strived to make my movements look decisive but I was sure, in truth, that I must have seemed suspicious. Disconnected concepts surged through my mind: can someone who replies immediately, without thought, be taken seriously; someone whose actions and notions were spontaneous rather than carefully considered; someone with predetermined ideas not open to discussion or flexibility? I could recall every detail of the group captain's conversation, of his no-nonsense approach, of how his mulish mentality had appeared to be stuck in the 1940s and 50s. Yet this was the 1960s; we had moved on; the world had changed for goodness sake. My one-sided talk with the senior officer had caused a small knot of apprehension to form in my stomach. I had even begun to feel a little sick. Wearied with the wait, though, I knew that I had to act.

A mosquito buzzed across my face while I continued to stride towards the hangar. I glanced up to see the moon's disapproving glower behind shrubs and olive trees. A ceaseless motion of autumnal leaves cast shadows upon a nearby wall. Through the gentle chill of the Cypriot night I heard the sound of voices. I could not stop or hide or turn around, that would have been absurd. I had to press on, to brazen it out if challenged. At a curve in the road I felt a hot needle of angst when I spotted some far-off figures. Then I thought I saw a person's shadow nearby as it moved in the darkness behind a wall. However, I still did not falter, though when I passed a row of huts with drab windows that obscured fearfully dark interiors, my instinct was to try to conceal, as if misdemeanour had been committed already, the specialist tool that I clutched in one hand: a long, flexible tube with a plunger that controlled a grab mechanism – like a fairground snatch device poised above kids' toys and sweeties. Although, just now, still technically innocent, I was nevertheless bent on skullduggery and perhaps this had stirred a guilty conscience.

The cause of this subterfuge, a recent fire-in-the-air suffered by a 29(F) Squadron Lightning aircraft, seemed to have produced problems of ever-growing complexity. The squadron, currently detached from RAF Wattisham in Suffolk to RAF Nicosia in Cyprus (the runway at Akrotiri, the usual base for Lightnings, was being resurfaced), was set to return home to Wattisham quite soon. As the squadron's junior engineering officer I had to oversee the serviceability of all the detached Lightnings for the flight home. However, the fire-in-the-air situation had thrown, one might say, a hefty and vexatious spanner in the works.

29 Squadron Lightnings at RAF Nicosia, Cyprus, October 1968.

I thought again of my interview with the group captain. Aged in my mid-twenties, I was a qualified engineering graduate recently promoted to the rank of flight lieutenant – achievements for which I had worked hard and felt quite proud. Yet the group captain's voice had reduced me instantly to a bogey-nosed five-year-old.

"That's not the way I do things, flight lieutenant," he had said. His eyes had flickered darkly.

"It's just that...sir..." the five-year-old's retort had petered out pitifully.

"This modern habit to rob or cannibalise parts from a serviceable aircraft in order to fix an unserviceable one merely creates long-term difficulties," the group captain had tiresomely, if correctly, pointed out.

"Under the circumstances, sir," the five-year-old had bleated, "could we not make an exception?" I had felt vulnerable to his disapproval.

"That's the trouble with your generation," the group captain had rattled on before I could marshal additional defences, "you just skate over the surface of things. You fail to grasp the long-term implications, to get to grips with underlying issues. Tutch..." like a policeman at a road junction he had held up his hand to thwart any further foolish response from the five-year-old. His big eyebrows had seemed to quiver. "Anyway," he had continued with a black look, "the answer is 'no' and that's final." Five-year-old had come to attention, offered his best military salute and retreated.

I had decided to return to the squadron via the officers' mess to mull over what to do next. The staff members in the mess, who spoke a curious mix of Greek Cypriot-English or Turkish-Cypriot English, had been outwardly pleasant though some had appeared to eye me with distrust. Maybe this was in my imagination, another twinge of guilty conscience sparked by the plot that had started to formulate in my head. A spare part, a hydraulic pipe, was needed for the fire-in-the-air Lightning, a part that was not available through normal channels in time for the squadron's return to Wattisham, a part that was specific and difficult to obtain. Another option, to be authorised to rob the required hydraulic pipe from a serviceable aircraft owned by the resident Lightning squadron, had been firmly ruled out. A further, more drastic, option – to ignore the good group captain, break into the appropriate hangar at night, locate the necessary pipe and make off with it – was now, as far as I could see, the only one open to me.

Oh well, I thought, what the hell? Some things had to be done the hard way.

As a first step, I decided to befriend the chief technician in charge of RAF Nicosia's deep maintenance unit. It did not take me long to locate him in the MU (maintenance unit) hangar. "Nice day," I said amiably as I walked up to him. He looked at me and frowned.

"Something you need, sir?" he asked.

"Yes...no...hmmm...what if?" I could hear my voice getting shrill.

"Sir?"

"I was wondering..." The chief technician's eyes lost focus then refocused. His jaw started to twitch. I was making him nervous.

Placed on the spot, I decided to explain all. As I began to relate details of the predicament, the chief technician warmed to the situation. At least, I thought, here's someone who remained open-minded. I managed to elicit the information that, as part of a modification programme, the adjacent Lightning was being stripped down, the part I needed had been removed and, indeed, I was probably standing close to it at that very moment.

"Any chance...?" I stared at him hopefully.

"Sorry, sir," he said. "No can do. The Groupie here has firm ideas about robbing aircraft parts."

"If you say so," I sighed peevishly.

No doubt looking glum, I judged that further dialogue was unlikely to be productive. I therefore thanked the chief technician for the information, made my excuses, and left.

Ha! I thought as I walked away from the MU hangar, time for the scheming to begin in earnest. In the shadowy kingdom of childhood, five-year-old was about to come up trumps. Either that or get himself court-martialled.

But the plan I had in mind offered no room for doubt. I would have to be resolute, innovative; recognise that this would be no easy ride. I was about to play a different game, an adult one with serious consequences.

I appreciated the need to try, as far as possible, to act and behave routinely. I dined in the officers' mess as usual, chatted with others, read the newspapers. The hour was therefore quite late when I departed from routine and left the mess to head for the hangar allocated to our squadron for the duration of the detachment. The heavy weight of potential hazards bore down on my shoulders like a storm cloud.

At the squadron hangar I sought out the night shift supervisor, a chief technician who I knew well. We talked about this and that until, to the chief technician's considerable surprise, I made for one of the specialist tool boards. I removed the mechanical fingers (the fairground grabber) plus a torch, placed appropriate 'tallies' over the shadow outline to indicate that the tools were in my possession, nodded a farewell to the ongoing amazement of the chiefie, then set off into the night.

Just now, with the mechanical fingers still thrust under my arm, worries about possible dangers persisted to swirl through my head. Ubiquitous crickets clacked away in Turkish/Greek Cypriot ciphers as if to add to my mental anguish. Invisible in the night hours, I could imagine the 6,400 feet towering, reproachful presence of Mount Olympus way off to the south and west of Nicosia. As I walked along and as moonlit shadows started to stress a sense of the surreal, irksome butterflies created havoc within my stomach. For Pete's sake, mid-twenties, qualified engineering graduate told himself, get a grip.

The maintenance unit hangar loomed. The bulky building, ominous-looking in the moonlight, was the object of my focus – the point of prospective success or disaster, and it lay ahead of me now. With each step I felt the butterflies intensify their antics. I was, at least, confident of one thing: I had checked that the maintenance unit team did not operate a night-shift; I had been assured that no personnel would be on duty. I should have the hangar to myself.

My first objective, to gain access, now presented a few possibilities. I scrutinised likely-looking windows, side doors and the great sliding doors at the building's front. I decided to concentrate on a side door. A smart push, a quick clout, and a shoulder, however, failed to budge the thing. I glanced up and down, left and right. Everywhere seemed quiet. There were no signs of the folk I had spotted earlier. I tried the door again. I fiddled with the handle, examined the surrounds, tinkered with the door lock. Get a grip, I remonstrated once more with myself, you're a non-five-year-old recently-promoted engineering genius. Suddenly I found a point of weakness: the lock looked rusty and somewhat ancient. Some persistent gentle persuasion, not to mention a less-than-gentle application of one size ten boot, and – hey presto! – the door gave way. I had gained access.

Aircraft hangars possess particular auras. Even in calm winds, doors and windows rattle incessantly as if in conversation. Perhaps they warned each other of impending peril, of an intruder within the premises. I switched on my torch and pointed the beam in different directions. The stripped-down Lightning remained on special jacks. Wires and pipes protruded, the engines lay to one side, panels had been left open. I sniffed the familiar odour of aircraft and associated machinery – a distinctive blend of fuel, rubber, oil, hydraulics. As far as practicable, I cupped one hand to conceal the torch beam; a light seen flashing through a window might cause an observer to raise the alarm.

My visit earlier in the day now proved useful. I had made a mental note of the maintenance unit's system to label and stow parts as the Lightning was dismantled. In typical air force style, the method and efficiency of this system was admirable. It certainly made my task easier. The hydraulic pipe I sought had a distinctive shape and, along with other items, had been locked inside a special cage protected by a wire mesh which, luckily, was of fairly open design. Judiciously, I shone the torch at an attached label and confirmed that this was, indeed, the part needed and that it had been classified as 'serviceable'. Brilliant, I thought, now for the mechanical fingers.

As any fairground user can testify, mechanical fingers will challenge the operator. Despite the most dextrous of efforts, the desired object, whether sweetie, cuddly toy or hydraulic pipe, can prove deceptively hard to grasp. I let out quiet curses of frustration while I struggled. With every move the wretched thing tried to slip this way and that – talk about get a grip, I mused. I was aware of the over-anxious thump of my heartbeat as I worked away. I listened out for extraneous sounds of danger but these were masked by my own heavy breathing and the hangar's perpetual, eerie rattles.

When, at last, I managed to gain a good grip, I eased the long pipe gently through the wire mesh. I placed the desired object carefully on the ground, re-arranged the remaining pipes to make them appear untampered-with, had a last, hasty glance around the hangar, then made for the side door as I grasped my prize. When closing the door behind me, I took trouble to leave the impression that, rather than intruder interference, the last person out had failed to lock-up properly.

It was not until I had returned to the mess for some much-needed sleep that the full significance of my actions struck me. A heady mix of exhilaration and exhaustion caused me to toss and turn in bed as the night's shenanigans replayed through my mind in slow motion, in rapid motion, then in dreadful, distorted dreams. The squadron would remain in Cyprus for a few days yet – time enough, I reckoned, for the proverbial to hit the fan.

At work the next day I quietly, quickly retrieved and adjusted relevant paperwork to transfer the priority demand for a new hydraulic pipe from 29 Squadron to the maintenance unit. I kept my profile low as preparations for the squadron's homebound flight progressed. I was especially keen not to cross paths with a certain group captain.

But I heard nothing more. As time went by, I retained, nonetheless, strong memories – even many decades later – of that fateful night. For one thing, I would recall with satisfaction the reaction of our squadron shift supervisor when I entered the hangar, strode up to him and handed over the hydraulic pipe. In turn, he gazed at me, at the hydraulic pipe, at the mechanical fingers, at the torch. We remained silent until, surreptitiously, I pointed towards the maintenance unit hangar. At this, he let out a long, low whistle of astonishment. "My God, sir," he breathed, "that's blatant daylight robbery."

"Not really," I replied with a shrug of the shoulders, "just a little night-time larceny."

He continued to stare at me for a moment or two but it was not long before a gleeful grin started to spread across his face.

(The fire-in-the-air mentioned in this chapter links with
The Lightning Boys *Chapter 7 – 'Ulp!')*

CHAPTER 7

CAN-DO LEGACY

ROGER BEAZLEY IN GERMANY

As I stood by the water's edge I'd gaze across the Möhne lake with a sense of the surreal. A shiver would go down my spine if I tried to picture the path taken by the Lancaster bombers of 617 Squadron. Struck by the painful clarity of the light, I'd screw up my eyes as I looked due south where sunlight would pick out the acres of trees that stretched towards the horizon. After a summer shower, a smell of pine resin, of warm earth by the dark waters of the lake, would evoke a haunting atmosphere. Sometimes, at weekends, I would walk around the area, observe the trees and wonder at the contrasts – at the gnarled and blackened ones, at the newer ones, tall, imposing. I would experience a curiously ethereal feeling as if the older trees had seen people like me hundreds of times, watched us come and go, could recall vividly the mighty night of 16/17th May 1943.

Twenty-five or so years on from that night there were usually plenty of folk, mainly tourists, who would stroll by the Möhne dam to examine the towers, the graceful curve of the dam's top, the repaired centre section that had been blown to smithereens by Wing Commander Guy Gibson and his fellow aircrew.

I was no German speaker, nonetheless I could imagine the troubled thoughts as people stared at the structure and I would speculate on the conversations:

"There, there look..."

"What's that?"

"It was a secret at the time."

"Where did they fly?"

"They flew in low at night. They faced tremendous anti-aircraft fire as they flew towards the dam."

"Crazy!"

"Courageous!"

From my base at RAF Gütersloh, where I was a member of 19(F) Squadron, the drive to the Möhnesee in my car did not take long, and for me, once there, the area held special significance. Shortly after I had joined the squadron in the summer of 1967, a new policy had been introduced: in addition to dealing with attacks by the Eastern Bloc's high altitude bombers such as the lumbering Tu-95 Bears or the less-lumbering Tu-22 supersonic Blinders, we were instructed to prepare for low level assaults too. A low altitude grid square system consequently was devised whereby each of our squadron pilots was allocated a particular square. My own personal, private grid square happened to coincide neatly with the surrounds of the Möhne lake. When I and the other pilots flew at a height of some 2,000 feet within our assigned grid squares in our Lightning Mark 2As, we would employ our airborne radars AI Mark 23 to look up for high level targets, and our eyeballs Mark 1 to look down for the low flyers.

When a Lightning needed more fuel, the pilot would whizz back to Gütersloh for a rapid turn round, staying in the cockpit before he rushed back to his allotted grid square. In his absence the grid square would remain unmanned but it was reckoned that the enemy bomber pilots, hardly privy to the fighters' timing, would be unable to adjust their own approach times appropriately.

Moreover, this grand strategy, if a little questionable, was in any case regretfully dwarfed by another, altogether larger, issue: come the 'big one', the Lightning pilots' thin blue line was likely to be overwhelmed by the Eastern masses that would appear from East Germany, Poland and the USSR bent on bombing the hell out of the West. As we struggled to provide defence against these hordes, it was reckoned by some so-called expert that individual Lightning pilots would have to contend with approximately 30 or 40 targets each. Under the circumstances, a brief absence from one's grid square for refuelling was seen, perhaps, as something of a detail.

With our squadron's interminable involvement in interminable exercises, and with the Möhnesee, so to speak, as my stomping ground, I became quite familiar with the locality. Sometimes, though, far from having to cope with overwhelming numbers, I might fly for ages around a grid square for the sake of just one or two spasmodic 'enemy' invaders. Long waits between targets could become tedious and the mind, therefore, might start to wander as one contemplated one's lot and as fanciful flights of imagination took hold. On a clear day I would look up to observe fragments of sky that glittered through the Lightning's canopy, I would look down to stare at the surface of the lake as I surmised if the fishing was good or whether a monster might lurk beneath and if so whether it could rival the fabled Loch Ness creature in which case it might suddenly surface to gobble up one of the many sailing boats that pottered around the lake. When I spotted the sailors gaze up as my Lightning roared past I would wonder if my presence was regarded as a sign of reassurance or an act of noisy nuisance. Some of the sailing folk would wave energetically, although I could never quite work out if the gesture was a friendly one or whether, *au contraire*, it was a signal to do something else. In either case, my wish to call out 'Hello sailor' was, unfortunately, impractical.

I conjectured whether a few of the older sailors might retain vivid memories of the night of 16/17th May 1943. When the first Lancaster bomber, flown by Wing Commander Gibson, released its bouncing bomb about 30 minutes after midnight on 17th May 1943, the bomb bounced three times and appeared to explode on target but failed to breach the dam. I could imagine the fear and sense of uncertainty felt by observers on the ground. I could imagine, too, the Lancaster crew's frustration when the skill and effort needed to hold exactly 60 feet above the water, to fly down to a bomb-release range of 400 yards from the dam, to maintain an accurate airspeed in the face of probing searchlights and relentless anti-aircraft flak...when the explosions of adjacent flak, the colours of tracer, the hollow *crumph* and blinding white flash and sudden blast of cold air when flak struck the Lancaster – and when sky was not sky but a confined space full of lights and violence and explosions that seemed impossible to penetrate, but the pilot and the six other members of crew would stay at their posts anyway as they braved the smoke and the flames and the danger and the gut-churning anxiety that was rapidly turning to terror...when all of that appeared to have been for nothing.

A further four attacks by other Lancasters ensued and it was during the last of these that the pilot, 23-year-old Flight Lieutenant David Maltby, saw the dam begin to disintegrate. Flight Lieutenant Maltby and his crew decided to drop their bomb anyway and the breach that followed, some 70 yards long and 20 yards high (and the repaired section still visible today), caused nearly 90% of the reservoir's waters to gush out. The flood water travelled 100 miles or so and caused severe damage and serious setbacks to Germany's war effort – testimony, among other matters, to the shortcomings in judgement of Harris, the head of Bomber Command who, just a few months before the operation, had declared: "This is tripe of the wildest description. There are so many 'ifs' and 'buts' that there is not the smallest chance of its working."

When I observed in broad daylight the night-time hazards faced by those valiant airmen I felt that, although no dambuster myself, I could empathise with their situation. "The conduct of your operations," Prime Minister Churchill had told Harris after the raid, "demonstrated the fiery, gallant spirit which animated your aircrews, and the high sense of duty of all ranks under your command." The author and actor Stephen Fry later wrote: '...these men were not just beefy chaps, they had real brains. Lancasters cannot take off at night in formation and fly at low level for hundreds of miles, drop an enormous bomb that is spinning at 500 revolutions per minute from exactly the right height and then move on to *another* target before returning home – all the time under fire from enemy anti-aircraft batteries – without a particular kind of steady, unblinking courage, tenacity and will that is out of the ordinary.'

The world may have changed out of all recognition since those dark 1940s' days but the endeavours and the fearsome loss of life suffered by the Lancaster crews has not been forgotten.

As I flew in my grid square above the Möhnesee I would listen out on the aircraft radio for information from the radar controller and from other Lightning pilots manning contiguous grid squares. I could picture, but not always see, my colleagues as they flew tidy lines in the sky while, like me, they waited for action that seemed painfully slow to materialise. The same could be said, I reckoned, for another of our duties, that of holding 'Battle Flight' at Gütersloh. With two Lightnings, two pilots and several back-up engineers on duty, the Battle Flight commitment generally involved hours of waiting around until, suddenly, an order to scramble would be followed by a burst of hectic activity. When this happened, the pilots would race up cockpit access ladders, snap into place a personal equipment connector for radio, oxygen and anti-g suit, strap in assisted by a member of groundcrew, and ensure that ejection seat safety pins were removed by the ground crewman. Then, when commanded by the controller, one or both aircraft would fire up their engines before taxy out and take-off. The whole process, from crew room to airborne, would take a mere matter of minutes, and usually less than the stipulated readiness state of five minutes.

About a year after joining the squadron I was assigned to Battle Flight one day when, to our astonishment, the two duty pilots were issued with 9mm revolvers and tin hats. Our eyes wide with incredulity, my fellow pilot and myself looked in turn at each other, at the revolvers and at the tin hats, but we remained uncertain whether to laugh or cry. It was August 1968 and we were told that the Soviet Union, worried about Czechoslovakian liberalisation under Dubcek's 'Prague Spring', had decided to invade that recalcitrant country. In Prague, citizens reproached the Soviet troops, engaged them in lengthy political dialogue, gave incorrect directions, removed road signs, refused to provide food or assistance. From our point of view, the powers-that-be at some HQ or other, agitated by these events, had decided that the solution lay in tin hats and pistols for the Lightning pilots. We did not, however, receive guidance on their use when airborne, neither were we sufficiently trustworthy, so it seemed, to be issued with actual bullets for the 9mm revolvers.

I think it was a member of our groundcrew team who, as he observed the pilots' bemused looks, picked up one of the tin hats, turned it over and over, placed it sideways on his head, flared his nostrils and rolled his eyes skywards in imitation of a Soviet bandit. "Laugh not," said my fellow pilot. "We're officially supposed to hate the Russians."

On another occasion, the Battle Flight Lightnings were brought to cockpit readiness following information about an unauthorised Hercules flight by an individual unqualified to fly the aircraft and thought to be intent on defecting to the East. Before long, I was scrambled to intercept the Hercules. I took up a south-easterly heading as ordered by the radar controller and my heartbeat began to race. The prospect of shooting down one of our own, albeit someone up to no good, was less than appealing. I ended up in a position well beyond my Möhnesee grid square and not far from the border with East Germany. After a thorough search of the area, however, I found nothing and was ordered to return to base. Later, I found out that the Hercules had ditched in the sea with the USAF technical sergeant still at the controls in his desperate, tragic attempt

19 Squadron Lightnings at RAF Gütersloh.

to return home to the USA from his base in England.

It was at about this time that, caught up in another exercise, I witnessed a situation which might almost have become a case of history repeating itself. Settled into my grid square routine, suddenly I picked up interesting information on the aircraft radio: low level target activity had been detected and it was heading my way. In an instant, any sense of lethargy was dispelled and I forgot concerns about a Möhnesee monster gobbling up sailors. I turned due east and manoeuvred to achieve a clear path between the autumn showers which had started to build up. From further chatter on the aircraft radio I learnt that several low level 'enemy' fast-jet fighter-bombers had passed through other grid squares. I searched anxiously as far ahead as the weather conditions allowed, but I saw nothing for a while.

I think it was the movement of a faint, fast shadow across the surface of the lake that I saw first. Then I discerned the target itself: a long, thin fuselage was flying at high speed across the lake directly towards the Möhne dam. I increased my airspeed and turned sharply to set up an interception profile. Initially, I tried to use adjacent cloud to conceal my position from the 'enemy' pilot and I took account of the sun's position. Before long, as I closed up from astern to missile-firing range, I was able to verify earlier suspicions: my 'enemy' was a F104 Starfighter and soon a good 'missile tone' in my headset confirmed that I was within firing range.

I don't remember exactly when it happened, but I recall the result vividly.

Visiting Danish pilots with pilots of 19(F) Squadron. Lightning pilots L-R: Bob Turbin, Laurie Jones, Peter Naz, Roger Beazley, Phil Williamson and Richard Pike.

As I pursued my target, I witnessed a vigorous evasive manoeuvre when, presumably, the pilot promptly realised that a fighter was on his tail. The F104 descended rapidly towards the lake's surface – so rapidly, in fact, that I held my breath in anticipation of impending disaster. Just at the last second, though, I saw the Starfighter's nose pitch up violently as the pilot recovered to a safe height. Nevertheless, the well-defined wake carved on the lake's surface suggested that the F104 had descended even lower than its Lancaster predecessors of a quarter century ago.

After this swift spurt of excitement, activity quietened again and a check of my fuel state dictated that I should return to Gütersloh soon. The rain showers persisted, some of them increasingly heavy, and I had to weave my way between the downpours in order to maintain visual contact with the ground. As I left the Möhnesee with its poignant atmosphere, I thought of the F104's close encounter of an unwelcome kind, of the curious link with those of the Lancasters of 617 Squadron. After the Lancasters' attack, the squadron was awarded a crest with the motto '*après moi le deluge*' – 'after me, the flood'. How appropriate, I reckoned, would have been my own squadron's motto before the attack: '*possunt quia posse videntur*' – 'they can because they think they can'.

CHAPTER 8

QUIET PLEASE!

BOB TURBIN LIKED TO MAKE HIS PRESENCE KNOWN

It was a casual enough enquiry. Even so, it took me by surprise when, one day in 1973, my boss asked me if I'd like to lead a four-ship display team for RAF Coltishall's Battle of Britain open day. When my astonished jaw had ceased its southerly drift, I gathered my wits to say: "Yes, sir. I'd like that very much."

"Okay," he said. "We'll adjust the daily flying programmes to give you time for rehearsals." Although our display would be non-aerobatic, we'd still need plenty of practice in order to achieve a high standard. The boss went on to name the other three pilots who'd make up the team and, before long, the four of us got together for a briefing.

"There's one small problem," I told the team members. "The station commander has decreed that we must not, repeat not, perform reheat rotation take-offs. Even though it's the Lightning's *pièce de résistance*, he reckons that the noise might upset onlookers." The reaction was woeful but unsurprising.

"Well I'll be darned," said number two. He adopted the vacant expression of cretins, though fortunately he did not dribble.

"I'm a Greek whatsisname," said number three querulously, but we were uncertain what he meant.

"I don't think I'll bother to come back," said the formation's number four as he smote his forehead with the heel of his palm and screwed up his face in an unattractive gesture.

"Calm down," I said. "We'll just have to make the best of it. Anyway, I have an idea."

"An idea?"

"A Turbin idea, no less."

I was, fortuitously, quite good at ideas – this was one of the nice things about me. Perhaps it was in part a consequence of my upbringing: from an early age I had been under the shadow of my two older brothers. One time, one of them had said to me: "Promise me, young Robert," he had scowled severely, "that whenever you are about to do something foolish, think of me, then don't do it." I do not recall my reaction to this but I do recall that, aged eleven years, I had won a scholarship to the Buckhurst Hill County High School in Essex and that I had followed my brothers when I became a pupil there.

At the age of 17 years and 10 months I had left with passes in two 'A' levels (English and French) and nine subjects in what today would be called, I believe, GCSE exams. My first job was with an advertising agency, although my main ambition at the time was to pursue a career as an operatic tenor. I was auditioned twice for Covent Garden with a third audition scheduled for early January 1956. At this point, National Service intervened and my call-up papers ordered me to report to the RAF Aircrew Selection Centre at Hornchurch. After success in the selection process I was sent to Canada for pilot training. Alas, however, at the end of my training I was told that no flying jobs were available for National Service aircrew. I therefore went back to the advertising industry to join a company whose offices, by good fortune, were in Kingsway, London, close to the RAF's recruitment headquarters. One day I was in this recruitment centre when, by chance, I met Air Marshal Sir Augustus Walker. The air marshal recognised me from my rugby days (he was a rugby referee) and asked me why I was out of uniform. When I explained, he nodded, looked wise and said: "Leave it to me." Within three months I was back in uniform and sent *post haste* to RAF Strubby in Lincolnshire for refresher training.

My first tour was on Hawker Hunter aircraft before, in 1962, I was posted to fly Lightnings with 74(F) Squadron. After 74 Squadron a variety of postings in the Lightning world ensued, including the Air Fighting Development Squadron at RAF Binbrook, a tour on 19(F) Squadron based at RAF Gütersloh in Germany, and 18 months spent with the Royal Saudi Air Force based at Dhahran in eastern Saudi Arabia. In September 1972, when posted to the Lightning Operational Conversion Unit at RAF Coltishall, I became an instructor with 65 Squadron.

All of this no doubt provided suitable background for the honour of leading the Lightning display team at Coltishall's 1973 open day. In any event, when I had explained to team members my bright idea to counter the anti-noise edict – my anti-anti-noise plan or AAN – my fellow pilots began to cheer up. However, I emphasised that details of the AAN plan would have to be kept quiet (ironically). This would not be difficult, though, as the initial practice sessions would be conducted away from the airfield. Later sessions would be over the airfield, but by that stage it would be too late to change our routine; the plan, therefore, should remain confidential until then.

The early practices went well and it was not until we had performed half-a-dozen or so further practices that calamity struck.

One day, having briefed my formation team, the four of us were keen to proceed. We had no hint of trouble at that stage. The August weather was good, our four Lightnings had been allocated, all was set. We walked out to the line hut together, signed individual aircraft logs then went to our separate aircraft.

Our procedures were slick, nonetheless as an instructor I was accustomed to carrying out thorough pre-flight and other checks; a 'kick the tyres, light the fires' mentality would not have set a good example to students. With the mighty voice of the Duke of Mantua from Verdi's Rigoletto humming through my head, if not my lips, I commenced the external checks on my Lightning Mk 1A. I felt in a good mood. I gaily checked that the protective cover had been removed from the Lightning's phallic-like pitot-static tube. I smiled indulgently as I verified that the engine intake was clear and that the radar dome looked undamaged.

As I moved back to check the starboard side of the aircraft, I did so with a spring in my step. I bent low to inspect the undercarriage mechanism and wheels; the Lightning's specially-made skinny tyres were expensive and prone to excessive wear in strong crosswinds so I examined them carefully. I stood up again and walked to the rear of the aircraft where, with a sense of awe, I stared up into the black wilderness of the aircraft's twin jet pipes set one above the other. What potency, what heat, what sheer brute force would be thrust through those massive pipes! Still humming happily, I checked the port side of the aircraft before I stepped up the boarding ladder hooked onto the cockpit side and clambered merrily into the cockpit.

A ground crewman now helped me to strap in before he removed the two ejection seat safety pins. When satisfied, he stepped down and unhooked the cockpit access ladder, then moved in front of the Lightning where a fire extinguisher had been pre-positioned. I went quickly through my pre-start checks before looking outside to monitor the other Lightnings. When all three pilots had given thumbs-up signs, I signalled the 'engine start' order.

Soon, with all four aircraft 'turning and burning' and ready to taxy out, I pressed my radio transmit button to speak with Coltishall air traffic control. The controller's tone seemed a little tense as he said "...formation...clear to taxy for runway..." A series of thumbs-up signs from the ground crewmen now indicated that wheel chocks had been removed. I therefore eased forward from my parked position, checked the function of the aircraft's brakes, then moved onto the main taxiway to lead the formation towards the take-off point.

Observed by the duty controller who was equipped with seriously enormous binoculars, the formation taxied past the air traffic control tower. A distant figure behind long panes of glass, the controller was conscious, perhaps, of his added responsibilities. In reply to my brusque request, his voice sounded anxiously high-pitched as he said: "...formation clear to line up and take off".

In deference to the ban on reheat rotation take-offs, I had briefed team members that numbers one, two and three should line up on the runway in a 'vic' (i.e inverted 'V') formation. Number four, meanwhile, would hold a wide 'finger four' position on the left side of the runway which he would maintain throughout the take-off run.

While I waited for the other pilots to take up position, I used the aircraft mirrors to observe their movements. When satisfied, I turned my head back briefly to confirm that number four was in place, then I looked ahead again. I had a last, hasty glance at my aircraft instruments; everything looked okay; we were ready. On the aircraft radio I called "rolling...GO!" and I released my aircraft brakes. Now I smoothly but firmly advanced both of my Lightning's throttles. As the formation began to thunder down the runway, my peripheral vision picked up a blur on each side. I knew that the others in the formation would be entirely focussed on my movements, I therefore made these as judicious as possible. At one hundred knots, all seemed fine. At one hundred and twenty knots, all was still fine. At one hundred and thirty-five knots I started to ease back the stick. It was just at that point, just as the Lightning's nosewheel began to lift, that trouble hit.

An almighty thump reverberated through the airframe as if a bullet had struck. The cause of the problem, however, was not a bullet but a large seagull. I felt a pronounced change of aircraft trim and I was aware of an altered engine note. A glance at the engine instruments revealed that both jet pipe temperatures had begun to rise rapidly into the gauges' red sectors. With my senses heightened by an adrenalin surge, I had to take a number of actions urgently. I instructed the other members to break formation. I transmitted an emergency call on the aircraft radio as, simultaneously, I eased back both throttles. Luckily, despite excessive jet pipe temperatures, the twin Rolls-Royce Avons continued to function and the Lightning still managed to climb. Gingerly, therefore, I turned the aircraft towards the downwind leg while I monitored the rate of climb.

Before long, as I turned the Lightning, I achieved an altitude of around one thousand feet on the downwind leg. I confirmed the cockpit indication of 'three greens' – the undercarriage was still down – and I carried out other pre-landing checks. I considered an attempt to jettison fuel but realised there was insufficient time. My paramount priority was to land the Lightning with minimum delay before one or both of the engines failed.

As I turned onto the finals leg, I experienced a sense of growing apprehension: a low level ejection would be inevitable if the engines failed at any stage. Perhaps with this in mind, I tried to avoid flying over property while I set up for the landing. My Rolls-Royce engines, however, did me proud. While I eased the aircraft towards the runway, the engines kept going and I was able to carry out a successful landing. Just after touchdown, I moved both throttles to the 'idle' position. As the Lightning slowed, I closed down both engines and brought the aircraft to a halt.

Fire trucks now raced up to the scene and fire crews provided ladders to assist with cockpit evacuation. One of the vehicles then drove me back to the squadron where, after debriefs and form-filling, I logged my shortest ever flight: three minutes.

Not long after this incident, further practice sessions were organised until, by the time of the big day itself, the team had worked up to a high standard. Nerves were taught, nevertheless, when we walked out to the aircraft for our Battle of Britain day display. The four Lightnings had been lined up in a special area. The machines gleamed in the September sun. Adoring crowds waved and cheered as the pilots performed external checks. When we clambered into our cockpits it was with a sense of high excitement. We started engines, taxied out and took off as briefed. We flew away from the airfield initially, then before long air traffic control cleared us to commence our routine.

While the main part of the display was good – great, even – the finale, by now known as Uncle Bob's P*ss Past or PP, was outstanding. The four Lightnings flew over the airfield in a box formation followed by a two-way split: numbers one and two broke right, numbers three and four broke left. Numbers two and three carried out an elongated 360-degree turn while lead and number four performed a ninety-degree turn followed by a 270-degree turn to position back over the display line in opposite directions calling contact with the other aircraft and on leader's command 'engage reheat' the idea was for numbers two and three to pass numbers one and four...or was it two and four to pass…? No matter; the point was this: our PP on that day made one hell of a lot of...NOISE.

CHAPTER 9

CHASING THE UNKNOWN

ALAN WINKLES' MYSTERIOUS SCRAMBLE

If the ghosts of time bear particular poignancy early in the year then the month of January 1968, in my own case, provided apposite evidence. It was the last day of the month and as a member of 5 (F) Squadron based at RAF Binbrook in Lincolnshire, and as a keen young Lightning pilot on my first tour, I was anxious for action even though, at first, such action seemed woefully absent on that day.

While I waited in the QRA hangar and while I listened to the steady tick of the 'Telebrief' device with its direct connection to the ground radar controller at Patrington, near Hull, I could not avoid a sense of impatience. Outside, the clear winter weather looked ideal for flying even if Binbrook's notorious winds persisted to whistle eerily through the hangar. The entire structure creaked and clattered as if in quarrelsome conversation with its surroundings. Fickle gusts would appear from nowhere, scoop up the remnants of autumn leaves, hustle them along while personnel caught in the open would wince when cold nipped at noses and pinched ears red.

In my small crew room I lounged languidly as I waited. I listened to the radio, read painful comment on the Vietcong's Tet Offensive in Vietnam's ongoing war, read the views of worthy individuals. I might even have checked alternative views of even worthier individuals in Hugh Hefner's mighty *Playboy* magazine. And I seem to recall that I nodded wryly when the radio presenter mentioned some droll quote about it being hard to get a man to understand something when his salary depended on him not understanding it.

5 Squadron at RAF Binbrook, March 1968. Alan Winkles fourth from the left.

My colleague that day was an experienced Lightning pilot but, despite the wintry winds, he had decided to work on a problem with his car which was parked by the QRA set-up. As a consequence, I had been nominated as 'Q1' (the first to fly in the event of a scramble order) while he held 'Q2'. Regardless of my best psychogenic efforts to urge the telebrief to say something of interest, time seemed to drag. The device's interminable, tiresome tick merely emphasised the morning's unhappy monotony. My sense of impatience was hardly helped when I thought about Lightning pilot colleagues based at RAF Leuchars in Scotland where frequent scrambles to intercept Soviet aircraft would produce remarkable and exciting tales to which we Binbrook-based fellows could only listen with envy.

It was while such thoughts swirled around my head that my pulse suddenly quickened and my mouth, I suspect, became as wide open as my eyes. The telebrief tick had stopped; a voice within now cried: "*Binbrook this is Patrington. Alert one Lightning.*"

I needed no further encouragement. I acknowledged the order, activated the scramble klaxon and dashed towards my aircraft. In nearly no time at all I skipped up the steps of the ladder on the side of the aircraft, wriggled slickly into the Martin Baker ejection seat and eased my bone dome (headset) over my ears. While I buckled up the seat straps I spoke with the Patrington controller. "Vector 130 degrees," said the controller without further preamble, "climb to angels one zero, call Neatishead on stud twelve...*scramble, scramble, scramble.*"

"Blimey!" I thought, barely able to believe my luck. In case the controller should change his mind, my procedures seemed even faster than normal as I confirmed the scramble details and signalled 'engine start' to the attendant groundcrew. The trusty Rolls-Royce Avons both sprang into life when, in sequence, I pressed the engine start buttons. Soon, I was taxying clear of the QRA hangar as I hastened towards the runway. "Clear for immediate take-off," said the air traffic controller at which, with a last glance around the 'office' to confirm completion of pre-take-off checks, I moved directly onto the runway, advanced the Lightning's throttles and felt the characteristic thump in the back as the aircraft accelerated.

As I climbed up that day I noted a hard, clear winter sun above immaculate 'CAVOK' conditions (cloud and visibility okay). To my left I glanced at the frost-covered confines of RAF North Coates, a surface-to-air missile station. I could make out four, out of a section of sixteen, Bloodhound missiles move steadily as they tracked my south-easterly course. This was an unusual heading; normally a scramble would have taken me north and east. I confirmed my heading, therefore, when I checked in with the controller at Neatishead, a radar unit in Suffolk. "Maintain 130 degrees," said the controller, followed simply and astonishingly by: "Buster".

"Buster?" I asked. The instruction meant 'full speed ahead' and with maximum reheat applied I would break through the sound barrier in a matter of seconds. As I was still over land, this would have created all kinds of damage and despondency below me.

"*Yes, buster. I repeat buster,*" said the controller urgently.

"Buster acknowledged," I said, though I thought to myself: okay, sunshine, whatever you say; on your head be it.

Soon speeding along like the proverbial cat on a hot tin roof (or some such expression), I was headed at supersonic airspeed towards the Wash and the north Norfolk coast. Suddenly, the controller changed his mind: "The target's slowing down," he cried. "He's in your twelve o'clock position, heading due west. His current range is 55 miles and he's slightly above you. Intercept and identify."

"Acknowledged," I said as, hastily, I cancelled both engines' reheats to curtail attendant problems of high fuel consumption. I turned the Lightning in order to offset the target to one side and decided to descend so as to place the incoming machine slightly above me. During the manoeuvres the Neatishead controller announced: "Your target is now very slow moving – about one hundred knots."

"One hundred knots?"

"Affirmative. And the target is still heading due west."

"Okay," I said, "one hundred knots copied." I swallowed hard and thought: 'damn'. My aircraft's stall speed was around 150 knots; this was going to be difficult.

At a range of 23 miles on my radar B-scope indicator I spotted the incoming target's 'blip'. Faint at first, the blip soon developed into a nice, fat radar return. I therefore called 'Judy' to the Neatishead controller, a codeword to declare that I would take over the intercept geometry: no further assistance required. I turned the Lightning to offset the target to the right-hand edge of my B-scope indicator and simultaneously I started to reduce airspeed. Initially, as I aimed for about 200 knots, all appeared to be working out. In a progressive turn onto the target's heading, and with ninety degrees to go, I decided to glance up from my B-scope; a truism in the Lightning world stipulated that one quick peep could be worth a score or more of radar sweeps. To my surprise, however, I saw nothing – not a dickey bird. Quickly, I re-buried my head in the B-scope's rubber shade in order to concentrate on the radar information.

With the blip still clearly indicated on the B-scope, I continued my turn until I rolled out at a range of approximately one mile behind the target. At this stage, at an altitude of some 14,000 feet, I was, as planned, slightly below the target. However, I was catching up fast – too fast. I therefore reduced my airspeed to 180 knots and initiated a weave; by allowing the target to drift out to an angle of about thirty degrees before a turn reversal, I further compensated for the disparity in airspeeds. At a range of 500 yards, just as the target crossed my centre-line, I looked up. I expected to see a small aircraft, a Cessna or some such machine, but I was mistaken. There was nothing there; the scene was blank; I was apparently alone in the sky.

"I've lost contact with the target," I said brusquely to the Neatishead controller.

"Understood...standby..." said the controller who then gave me a series of instructions. Within just thirty or so seconds the target's clear, plump blip had returned to my B-scope.

"I've regained contact," I said. "Has the target started to accelerate?"

"Affirmative," said the controller. With a small sense of relief, I realised that this should make the next visident (visual identification) easier. I advanced the Lightning's throttles and continued to follow my B-scope indications. The procedures went smoothly enough and soon, as I closed up once again to a range of 500 yards, I looked up to see what was there. As before, however, I saw not a thing. This cannot go on, I thought; it's crazy; the situation was humiliating – absurd; it seemed like a trap...an enigma that gnawed at the mind's division between fantasy and reality so that almost anything became possible. It was as if mirages in the sky were fighting battles amid illusory creatures and unidentified flying objects. I even adjusted the height of my seat in vague, fruitless attempts to place whatever or whoever was there against a backdrop of sea.

A third, and final attempt was equally unsuccessful, after which the controller ordered me to return to base. I felt very downhearted; I'd done my best but I'd failed. Worse still, I could offer no explanation for the failure. Perhaps Neatishead regarded me as some kind of pariah pilot – a feeling that was hardly helped when I heard the other QRA pilot, the more experienced Lightning man, check in on the aircraft radio. Neatishead had scrambled the 'Q2' Lightning to offer a second opinion in this strange situation.

It was about an hour later that my colleague returned. As he entered the small QRA crew room his expression revealed a mix of irritation and perplexity. He shrugged in reply to my enquiring look. "Didn't see a bloody thing," he said tersely. "Like you, I just ended up chasing my tail."

I was about to respond when I felt a gust of cold air on my back. A window had blown open and an icy Binbrook blast had begun to rush in.

"I'll close it," said my colleague.

"Don't worry, I'll do it."

In a couple of strides I crossed the room to where the window had swung on its steel frame. As I grabbed the window handle I stared for a moment at the airfield's open expanse, the bleak Lincolnshire acres beyond. Somewhere, far away, I thought I heard an unusual sound, like the hum of an engine, but it might have been in my imagination. I tried to make out the source but saw nothing so I closed the window and turned round. As I turned, a sharp, spontaneous shudder went down my spine. I noticed that my colleague's face had grown uncommonly pale. It was almost as if he had seen a ghost.

CHAPTER 10

MAD MOMENTS

Simon Morris sitting in a 92 Squadron Lightning cockpit, early 1970s.

SIMON MORRIS PUSHING THE BOUNDARIES

The mind, it seems, likes to play tricks in situations of high anxiety. It is as if, in dire scenarios, the brain thinks that it might be best to detach itself from reality. Simultaneously, memory cells will go into overdrive after which details can be recalled with uncanny clarity. Alarming scenes will run through in front of the eyes as though watching a dramatic film so that the event may be remembered, even many years later, as if it had occurred only yesterday.

In my own case, the circumstances that had led to such a state were as unforeseen as they were perilous. One moment I was in a position of good order and control while I flew my instrument rating test until, following a few minutes of sheer, unadulterated madness, the aircraft and the lives of its two pilots and many others on the ground below were in jeopardy. Despite this, when I heard my examiner's agitated voice call: "*prepare to eject*," for some inexplicable reason his words caused me to relax. To some folk, as our two-seat Lightning T4 spun ever downwards towards a busy German town, such a call might have appeared not only superfluous but also the cause of even greater suspense within our cockpit. For me, however, the instructor's words seemed to formalise the situation: now I felt free to release the bottom ejection seat handle which I had been gripping almost guiltily and to reach up for the main ejection seat handle above my head. I waited for his command: "eject!" which surely would come at any moment. Meanwhile, perhaps in part because of my curious and entirely illogical sense of sudden relaxation, my mind appeared to drift in remarkable and random directions as if I needed desperately to justify to myself why I had ended up in such a position.

For one thing, I should not really have been a member of Her Majesty's Royal Air Force. I was what might have been described as a wild colonial boy when, three years earlier in 1970, I'd arrived at London's Heathrow Airport to be greeted with suspicion by the immigration officer. Born in England on 13th May 1950, my home was in Dar es Salaam, Tanganyika (now Tanzania) where my father was a civil engineer. Consequently, I'd held what was known as a British Overseas passport. The immigration officer had adopted a peculiar expression, something between a sneer and a challenge, when he'd looked me up and down. A group of RAF policemen standing behind him had gazed in my direction but had remained impassive. The immigration officer had frowned as he asked me how long I intended to stay and whether I planned to seek employment. "I'm going to join the Royal Air Force," I'd said, glancing hopefully at the RAF policemen, although their facial expressions hardly radiated encouraging moral support. A few further questions had followed after which the immigration officer had grunted some comment, then waved me through.

My intention to join the Royal Air Force, though, had been genuine enough. However, some years before this, when at the King's School, Rochester in Kent, where I'd been a boarder and where I'd started my military life as a member of the army section of the school's Combined Cadet Force, my reasons for changing to a light blue uniform had been less than glamorous. One day, our squad corporal had seemed to smirk as he gave the order: "all those who fancy becoming a 'crab' by joining the RAF section, fall out." One or two individuals had sneaked off while the rest of us had cast sideways glances to see who had gone. Meantime, our squad corporal, an odious fellow who I'd disliked heartily, had reached out to shove me sideways to fill a gap. He'd called me an idiot for moving too slowly. At this, I'd performed a smart right turn, saluted and marched off towards the light blue yonder even though I had not the faintest idea what was involved and, in any case, had cared not a jot as my entire aim was to irritate that tiresome squad corporal even more than he was irritated already.

A year or two later, by which time I'd been promoted to the rank of cadet flight sergeant and had gained some gliding experience, I'd applied for a Royal Air Force scholarship. This had seemed a natural progression although, in truth, I had no real ambition to join the RAF or to become a pilot. I had wanted to be a civil engineer, like my father. Nonetheless, out of some 4,000 applicants I was one of the lucky few (four, I was told) to be selected. Problems persisted, however, when I failed my RAF medical test with 'low tone hearing loss in the left ear'. A further test at the Central Medical Establishment had confirmed the finding. "Suppose I'd better become a nav, then," I'd said to the doctor.

"No chance, old son. Navigators need to have good hearing to understand what their pilots say."

"Air Traffic Control?"

"Nope. It's the equipment branch or engineering for you."

"What?"

"It's the equipment branch or…" he'd raised his voice.

"I heard you the first time."

"Oh."

"Come on, Doc. Have a heart."

"Sorry, old chap. It's out of my hands."

I'd stared gloomily at the doctor as he gathered up the medical notes. "Now where on earth should I send all this ghastly paperwork?" he'd begun to grumble to himself. "Back to Biggin Hill, I suppose."

"I'll take it for you, doctor," I'd volunteered. "I'm on my way to Biggin Hill now," I'd lied.

"Okay, then. Why not? That will be helpful." He had seemed grateful for the offer.

I had left the medical set-up feeling thoroughly downhearted. I'd decided to catch the Tube to Marble Arch before wandering unhappily around Hyde Park while I contemplated my future. I'd continued to clutch the good doctor's paperwork as, darkly, I pondered the unkindness of the fates. Eventually, I suppose, it was inevitable that discretion, even if the better part of valour (according to Mr Shakespeare's theory), should give way to curiosity. I'd sat down on a bench and stared at the envelope marked 'Medical-in-Confidence'. I'd turned the package over, given it an expeditious shake, even listened (with my good ear) for possible alien interference. I had glanced left and right to ensure that

I was not overlooked, then ripped open the envelope. The contents, I'd quickly determined, were not worth the paper they were written on. I had no alternative, therefore, but to file the whole package as neatly as possible in the nearest wastepaper bin. I then left Hyde Park to set off back to East Africa post haste as any well-behaved, non-wild colonial boy should do.

It was some months later that my parents received a letter from the RAF asking why I'd not taken up my place at Cranwell. After further letter exchanges I was summonsed back to London for another audiometry test. This time, when in the acoustic chamber, I had kept pressing the test button even after the tone was too faint for me to hear it. In fact I was still pressing the button when the door was opened and a young airwoman had taken off my earphones and said: "It's okay, sir – all over now." She had gone on to confirm that I had passed the test with absolutely no indication of hearing loss in either ear. (This technique, by the way, subsequently got me through 40 or so years' worth of audiometry tests. Nowadays I wear hearing aids, nevertheless I remain confident that I could pass an audiometry test without difficulty. The moral is simple: don't give up; keep pressing the button. That's the way to do it.)

My flying training had commenced shortly after this and I had been lucky to pass both the basic and the advanced training courses as one of the top students. During the course we were handed forms that asked for our first three choices of aircraft posting. I'd put simply: 'Lightning, Lightning, Lightning'. I had felt more than delighted, therefore, when, on my 23rd birthday, I'd arrived at RAF Coltishall to attend the Lightning Operational Conversion Unit.

One thing we learnt swiftly at Coltishall was that the Lightning's characteristics in a spin were erratic and hazardous. It was prohibited to enter a spin deliberately in a Lightning. In the event of an inadvertent spin, stated the Pilots' Notes, the aircraft should be abandoned by a minimum height of 10,000 feet.

This dictum was no doubt in my mind on Christmas Eve 1973 as our Lightning T4, still in a violent spin as the aircraft passed through 5,000 feet, continued to plunge downwards directly above the centre of Herford, an historic, pristine town founded by Charlemagne and situated in the prosperous German state of Nordrhine-Westfalen. By now my examiner had cried: "prepare to eject!" My hands had reached up to grasp the top ejection seat handle.

Such an improbable – incredible – situation had been sparked just a few minutes earlier when the ground controller had advised us: "there's an aircraft, similar type to yourselves, in your one o'clock position at a range of five miles."

"I have control," the examiner said to me as he grabbed our Lightning T4's flight controls and concurrently selected reheat on both engines. Normally a placid enough fellow, he at that second appeared to undergo prompt transmogrification. Evidently irresistible, so it seemed, was the temptation to engage in a brief dogfight with a Lightning from our rival squadron. In practically no time, with high levels of 'g' as the two aircraft had wheeled about the sky, we ended up in a classic Battle of Britain scenario: two pilots both determined to outdo their opponent. The battle of the 'top guns', though, did not last long. After some violent manoeuvres during which both aircraft were pushed and pulled, turned and rolled, climbed and dived, it was our Lightning which managed to achieve a position of advantage above and behind the adversary, and within missile firing range. Less advantageous, however, was our airspeed. I hardly needed to look at the airspeed indicator gauge. The unstable, wallowing motion of the aircraft revealed clearly enough that we were close to stall speed.

After that, events began to happen fast. Our Lightning T4 appeared to quiver for a second or two, as if in a flutter of uncertainty. Then, in an abrupt and vicious sideways movement, the aircraft flicked into an incipient spin. The nose dropped to a very steep nose-down attitude and, with the airspeed close to zero, the Lightning entered the autorotational stage of a fully developed spin.

Just now, with the Lightning still hurtling downwards, ongoing thoughts persisted to rush through my head in haphazard fashion. A detached voice tried to speak to me: "*Now Simon, you musn't do this...no, no Simon, you shouldn't be doing this...definitely not, Simon don't do it...*" A hideous figure swam before my eyes, the body and limbs swathed in plaster, the frog mouth set in a rictus grin that revealed the stubs of several teeth. Like an irresponsible schoolboy who had committed some crime and was bound to be found out, I glanced guiltily around me. Scattered clouds, some light-coloured, some dark, chased each other in small circles; they ran dizzily faster and faster – the light then the dark then the light then the dark; I felt helpless, mesmerised into inactivity like a creature caught in the glare of a car's headlights. In place of the cold, December day's reality I fantasised about blazing sunshine, a huge hot sky, and below on all sides great stretches of desert scrub overlooked by Mount Kilimanjaro in the northern reaches of my home country. I imagined a calm evening with small wisps of white cloud motionless above. I pictured a cosy bedroom with a vase of roses on a table by the bed.

Our altitude was now some 2,000 feet above ground level. I became suddenly very tired and very hot. Perspiration started to run down my face. Clouds, dark and light, still chased each other in rapid, giddy circles. Perhaps that odious corporal was right after all; maybe I should not have become a 'crab' – I should have stayed as a 'pongo', stuck with the boring old army. This was no place for a wild colonial boy, let alone a well-behaved, non-wild one. I had been tryingly trained – brainwashed – by the air force's military machine and it was all going seriously pear shaped.

At 1,000 feet, with my grip on the ejection seat handle becoming ever tighter, I sensed the culmination of my state of icy, paralysed calm. I could see unwelcome, outlandish items pop into view: faces staring up, a church spire, spots on the Lightning's windshield, houses all around, rows of parked cars, the Lightning's shadow fleetingly silhouetted against a building, a tall tree with trimmed arms that stood black against bright Christmas decorations. I was aware of my examiner's shrill utterances as he muttered endlessly, agonisingly, to himself, pattering his way through spin recovery actions.

Suddenly, at the very nadir of my mental gyrations (not to mention the physical gyrations of the Lightning), a small glimmer of hope dawned. By now the aircraft was at ultra-low level with a nose-up attitude of 40 degrees (yes, forty degrees). Both engines were at full reheat as they blasted flames, fumes and fury at magnitude 10-plus on the Richter scale along the length and breadth of Herford's ancient, pristine main street. The Lightning's spin, however, had been brought under control. The aircraft appeared to hang in the sky like a puppet suspended on strings. Time and motion seemed to stop. Gradually, though, as the massive might of the Lightning's twin Rolls-Royce Avon engines persevered with their struggle against gravity, the Avons started to gain the upper hand.

Now, as the Lightning accelerated at an exponential rate, the airspeed and the altitude swiftly began to look healthier again. From our calamitous, ground level situation we were suddenly back up at 10,000 feet as if propelled there by a giant spring...instant deliverance from chaos and insanity, potential death and destruction. It was hard to take in. For a second I wondered if the experience had actually happened; perhaps I had dreamed the whole thing; maybe it had been a mere flight of fancy. I glanced at my colleague. Despite his close-fitting oxygen mask, the sheet-white pallor of his face revealed his state of shock. I shook my head; so the episode had not been a dream after all; pity! The instrument rating examiner, though, seemed in a sorry plight, one of acute torpor – a psychiatric reaction as if, within the petrified passages of his brain, the narrowness of our escape was being played over and over like some interminable horror movie. I preferred not to speculate too closely on the intense mix of agitation and dread that must have been charging through his head.

"Would you like me to take control of the aircraft?" I asked him. He nodded a 'yes' but said nothing. I grasped the Lightning's flight controls, disengaged reheat, spoke politely to air traffic control and elected for a visual recovery to our base at RAF Gütersloh. Throughout this procedure, while I headed back for a landing which I attempted to make as innocuous-looking as possible, he maintained a stunned silence.

It was later that evening, when he'd recovered his voice, that an impromptu meeting with my instrument rating examiner took place in the officers' mess. His expression suggested that he was still a worried man. Our Lightning T4 had exceeded allowable 'g' limits and had been declared unserviceable while the engineers completed safety checks. We had not, however, revealed details of our involuntary spin.

In the officers' mess I was joined by my girlfriend who, along with her sister, had chanced to be Christmas shopping in Herford at the time of the incident. They had witnessed the whole terrifying ordeal as our Lightning had plummeted towards them.

If conversation was awkward initially, it was not long before my girlfriend decided to be direct. "What do you have against my boyfriend," she said staring into the instrument rating examiner's troubled eyes, "that would make you wish to finish him off?" She spoke softly so as not to be overheard by others in the room.

He mumbled some reply.

My girlfriend, though, seemed dissatisfied. "You remember what happened?" she hissed, a touch of sarcasm in her tone.

"Yes, I remember," he said. "A rush of blood to the head – a mad moment – something I shall never forget. Sorry."

An uncomfortable hush ensued.

"My God," she said eventually. "Someone up there must have been keeping a kindly eye on you two." She pointed first at us, then heavenwards.

She was right, of course. There was no doubt that we had been treated with astonishing benevolence by the deity – more so, perhaps, than we deserved. Despite that, details of the episode remained confidential within our small group; other than amongst ourselves and close friends, my girlfriend and her sister did not talk about the near-disaster that they had observed. No complaints were received from the German authorities. No individual citizens submitted any form of censure even though many hundreds of Christmas shoppers must have witnessed the scene. The tale of that brief moment of madness appeared to become lost in the mists of time. Until, that is, today.

FROM ARDUA TO ASTRA

If my spinning incident had plumbed the depths, it was some two-and-a-half years later that I had an opportunity to examine the opposite end of the spectrum.

It was early in the morning on 28th July 1976 when I made preparations for a Lightning T4 air test. The aircraft had undergone deep maintenance and the engineers had requested an air test before the machine could be 'signed off'. A planned schedule had to be followed so I quickly went through the paperwork to remind myself of the requirements. These included an accurately timed, level acceleration from Mach 0.9 to Mach 1.7 at an altitude of 40,000 feet. The workload would be high, the fuel consumption would be high – in fact everything would be high, especially in the T4 trainer with its small ventral fuel tank.

When I walked out to the aircraft, I went via the engineering set-up to sign for the Lightning and to speak with the duty engineers. "Should be no problem, sir," said the chief technician. "We've strapped up the right-hand seat. The preflight's been done. The paperwork's in order. She's all ready for you."

"Thanks, chief." I scrawled a signature then set off for the Lightning T4 XM 955. While I walked towards the aircraft, a peculiar sensation – as buoyant as a bubble – appeared to come over me. As if by some strange premonitional process, I seemed to know that something exceptional would happen on this flight.

When near the Lightning T4, my by-then experienced eye confirmed that the radar dome and canopy area looked okay. I checked that the pitot tube's cover had been removed, then felt along the length of that symbol of virility which appeared to challenge those who dared to inspect it too closely. I smiled coyly to myself when I remembered my own personal, private experience of Lightning pitot tubes. This, I recalled, went back some years, to my first inflight refuelling sortie. That sortie had not gone well; I'd struggled to apply the correct techniques and at one point my aircraft had ended up within the powerful air vortices formed behind a Victor tanker's wing. The result had been dramatic: my Lightning, pounded by the violent airstreams, had ended up in an undemanded, vertical dive (these seemed to become habit-forming during my Lightning career) with, before long, an indicated airspeed of 800 knots as the aircraft plunged earthwards.

My thoughts as the machine plunged were along the lines of 'flipping marvellous', although it might not have been the word 'flipping'. On this occasion, however, the Lightning was not in a spin; recovery had been relatively straightforward and I'd soon managed to climb back up to rejoin the Victor tanker. Unfortunately, my airspeed indicator gauge had remained stuck at 800 knots. When I'd reported this to the pilot of the other Lightning, still quietly practising his own in-flight refuelling skills while I'd gone plunge-about, he'd moved into a close formation position on my aircraft for a visual inspection. "It's your pitot tube," he'd said at length, "it's bent downwards and backwards through almost 180 degrees."

"Bent pitot tube?"

"Bent as a bad bastard on a bank raid."

"Say again?"

"I say again...it's bent."

"Hey-ho." The news had caused implications to brush across the surface of my brain. A weak point in the construction must have buckled during the violent manoeuvres. Further in-flight refuelling would have been impractical; I'd needed to get back to base ASAP.

"I'll lead you down," my Lightning colleague had said.

I'd experienced no difficulty during the subsequent recovery and landing, and later that day I had asked if I could keep the bent pitot tube as a memento. "No problem," my boss, Wing Commander Chris Bruce, had said, and to this day the device remains in my house in Canada where it makes an ideal lamp stand.

However, for the portentous day of the air test itself, when, carefully, I scrutinised the Lightning T4's pitot tube, I was conscious of its significance for the accurate airspeed and altitude readings required. When satisfied, I moved back to examine the starboard undercarriage system, the underwing surface, and the airframe sides before I walked to the rear of the aircraft to inspect the jet pipe area. Soon, on completion of the external checks, I clambered up the cockpit access ladder on the left side of the two-seat aircraft.

As I strapped in, I glanced at the adjacent German countryside. Flat farmland stretched beyond the boundary fence of RAF Gütersloh; further away, highlighted on the horizon, I could make out lines of pine trees. The air traffic control tower, daubed in green camouflage paint, was positioned some distance from the runway. The runway itself, which stood out as a black ribbon of tarmac surrounded by grass, had been reinforced and lengthened to cope with Lightning operations.

I reflected for a moment on the sense of familiarity I now enjoyed here in Germany, although in some respects this could seem inappropriate. Set in the heart of West Germany's most populous and most economically powerful state, RAF Gütersloh was close (a mere matter of minutes of flying time in a Lightning) to the hazards created by the iniquitous Inner German Border, the dreaded 'iron curtain' that divided the West from the East. As a consequence, the attitude of local folk to our noisy flying activity was, in general, one of tolerance – considerably more so than at home in the United Kingdom. Even so, we avoided flying at supersonic airspeeds outside a specially designated and less well-populated area due north of Gütersloh. This was the area I would use for today's air test.

With my engine start procedures completed, I scribbled down notes on the special kneeboard that carried the air test schedule. I asked air traffic control for taxy clearance, then tested the aircraft brakes before I set off for the runway-in-use. Conscious of the Lightning T4's limited fuel reserves, I taxied at a reasonably rapid pace. In my mind, I tried to go over the required performance details during the take-off run; these would be needed by the engineers in their post-flight air test report. Soon, as I approached the runway, the controller cleared me for immediate take-off. I moved swiftly towards the take-off point before, with the Lightning's wheelbrakes applied, I advanced the Rolls-Royce Avon engines to around 80% power. On the air test schedule I recorded temperatures, pressures and other key information. Then, having double-checked the remaining pre-take-offs, I advanced the twin throttles to full power as, simultaneously, I released the aircraft brakes.

As the Lightning T4 roared off down the runway, I made a mental note of the aircraft's performance figures. When settled in the climb, I wrote these down while I headed due north towards Hamburg. I planned to fly to the northern edge of the supersonic area before heading south for the supersonic run. The Lightning T4's forward fuselage cross-section, with distinctive bulges to accommodate the side-by-side crew, offered an improved 'area-rule' (transonic drag reduction) profile. On top of this, the lack of an in-flight refuelling probe, a small ventral fuel tank and no missiles all added to what was known as a 'hot ship' – hotter, indeed, than other marks of Lightning.

Before long, as I rolled out on the planned southerly heading, I trimmed the aircraft at an accurate altitude of 40,000 feet with the Machmeter indicating exactly 0.9 Mach. There was no time to waste. I'd already spoken to the controller, so I re-checked, visually and on my airborne radar, that all looked clear ahead then I engaged full reheat on both engines. The Machmeter soon reacted: Mach 1.0...Mach 1.3...Mach 1.5. At this altitude there were no outside references to offer an impression of speed so I had to rely on the Machmeter alone to indicate progress. The acceleration did not take long; in just a couple of minutes or so the required Mach 1.7 was indicated on the gauge. Suddenly, it occurred to me that a good distance lay ahead before I reached the limit of the designated supersonic area; the Lightning could remain at this airspeed with impunity for a while yet. Why not use the opportunity, I thought, for a small experiment of my own?

Without further ado, I hauled back the Lightning T4's control stick. My eyes narrowed as I scanned the 'g' meter to hold a steady 4 'g' for a short period. Then I applied a small forward movement of the stick to maintain a nose-up angle of 85 degrees. Now, as the Lightning began to hurtle upwards with no bother at all, I carefully watched my altimeter: 45,000 feet...50,000 feet...55,000 feet. At a reading of 55,000 feet it occurred to me that in the event of aircraft pressurisation failure I could face problems. Even though I could switch to 100 per cent oxygen at a pressure of 50 Hg, and even though I was wearing a full pressure jerkin, potential trouble still loomed. I decided, therefore, to roll the Lightning on to its back to help restrain the rate of climb. I soon discovered, however, that the rate of roll at these high altitudes was slow – painfully slow. At more normal heights, the slightest movement of the ailerons would cause the Lightning to roll through 360 degrees almost before you'd realised it. That day, up there, matters were different.

As the aircraft persisted with its upward trajectory, I still monitored the altimeter closely: 60,000 feet...65,000 feet. Suddenly I realised that I was close to 70,000 feet. Like some exuberant ballistic missile on a determined run, the Lightning T4 kept going although I recall that the rate of climb eventually started to reduce. With the aircraft some thirteen miles above the surface of the earth I was well into the stratosphere, but I saw with relief that my airspeed did not reduce below 180 knots which equated to 0.9 Mach.

The sensation at that high altitude was surreal, even eerie. Through the top of my canopy (remember I was upside down) I could distinguish most of the landmass of Germany. The sky, the colour of deep blue – almost black – ink, formed a vast backdrop to the distinct line of the earth's curvature. A great distance below I observed scattered patches of white cloud which produced dazzling, bizarre reflections. I experienced a strong sense of awe for the intoxicating beauty and brilliance of the views around me. The situation was unique. My surroundings, though, were bleak, alien; I was in a world of silence and loneliness to which I did not belong; I began to feel an urge to return to civilisation without delay.

A glance at my engine instruments confirmed that both of the Rolls-Royce Avon's reheats remained lit, although they had reduced from full reheat to stage four. Acutely aware of the need to avoid engine flame-out, I decided not to touch the throttles for the time being. The flight controls still felt sluggish and unresponsive so I elected to make minimal control inputs. At length, however, as the aircraft began to descend, I judiciously rolled the wings level and selected a suitable heading for home.

With my recovery to Gütersloh now underway, I could mull over my exceptional experience. I knew that I couldn't claim the Lightning's high altitude record; others had flown to greater heights than me. Even so, the event would mark, in one sense at least, the personal pinnacle of my career – a 37-year flying career during which I would fly 40 different aircraft types. (On leaving the RAF after 12 years' service, I'd become a company pilot for two years, then serve with the Republic of Singapore Air Force for a brief spell before joining British Airways where eventually I'd become a senior captain on the Boeing 777.)

Just now, with my mind still contemplating the recent spontaneous, implausible experience, I struggled to work out the ramifications. I felt as if I had witnessed a magnificent concert; an audience of one transported to a particular place; an intensely privileged place, a place of euphoria. I could hardly claim to be an astronaut, nonetheless I was conscious of comments made by astronauts, of the clean and pure sensation inclined to touch the soul as planet Earth was observed from afar.

If such thoughts seemed high-flown, it was not long before I was brought back to reality when, after an uneventful landing at Gütersloh, I discussed the air test results with engineers. We went over the figures, re-checked the air test schedule, discussed this and that. "Thanks, sir," said the chief technician eventually.

"No problem," I said, and turned around to head for the operations set-up and a much needed cup of coffee. As I walked, an eclectic mix of thoughts beyond the nitty-gritty of air test schedules persisted to surge through my mind. My eyes had been opened. I had raised my gaze to the heavens. The wild colonial boy had been taken to new boundaries – *per ardua ad astra*. But for the time being, I reckoned, the wild colonial boy had landed – Apollo 11 was down – one small step for man, one giant leap for my Lightning T4. Now I felt dog tired and very hungry. I had a deep sense of satisfaction too.

CHAPTER 11

A CAREER INSPIRATION

DR RICHARD MARSH LAUDS THE P1'S LEGACY

"*Mayday, Mayday*...this is Skybus 1...I am under attack from 6 Soviet MiGs...*Mayday Mayday*."

When I heard this call, I was flying my English Electric P1B at just below the speed of sound along the East German border. It was the period of the Cold War, sometime in the mid-1950s and I knew that Skybus 1 was a lumbering NATO troop transporter en route to Berlin.

I replied immediately – "Hello Skybus 1. This is Tiger Leader altering course to intercept the enemy." Without any concern for my own safety, I slammed the throttles forward to engage full reheat, accelerated to Mach 2.5 and did a fairly improbable 15g right turn towards the enemy. Moments later I caught sight of Skybus 1. Smoke was streaming from the transport aircraft's engines and six MiGs were buzzing around it. "*Tally Ho...Tally Ho... bandits dead ahead*," I shouted excitedly on the aircraft radio as, with my two 30mm cannon armed and ready to fire, I closed in.

Then disaster struck: I hurtled at high speed into an elderly pair of female knees. There was a yelp and a cup of hot tea descended over my head and onto my precious English Electric P1 balsa wood model. My severe and unforgiving maiden aunt was far from amused and she turned to my mother and said: "Apart from being a terrorist, what is young Richard going to do when he grows up?"

My mother pondered this question as she mopped up tea and soggy biscuits from the carpet and said: "Can't you see – either he's going to fly aeroplanes or build them. He's absolutely mad about the things."

My mother's prediction was prescient. Just over a decade later, in 1967, as a raw young engineering graduate I presented myself at the gates of Filton House in Bristol to join the British Aircraft Corporation's Concorde design team. Looking back nearly half a century later I have no doubt that one of the principal inspirations in my choice of career was that remarkable range of aeroplanes from English Electric Aviation Limited: the P1A and the P1B which evolved into the Lightning fighter.

The biplane Gloster Gladiator was still in front-line service with the Royal Air Force in 1940. In 1947 the Ministry of Supply produced Experimental Requirement 103 which led directly to Britain's only supersonic fighter of the era – just seven short years from biplanes being used in combat to the requirement for an aircraft which, with modern engines and avionics, would still be a serious contender in the 21st century; quite astonishing.

English Electric was one of the founder companies of the British Aircraft Corporation, and the men primarily responsible for the P1 and the Lightning were W E W 'Teddy' Petter (also father of the Canberra and the Gnat), Freddie (later Sir Frederick) Page, and a brilliant aerodynamicist called Ray Creasey. During my happy career on the Concorde Supersonic Transport (SST) project I came to realise just how much of the Lightning's DNA had percolated through to our magnificent Concorde machine. This was apparent not only in the aerodynamics, structures and systems of Concorde, but also in the way we went about conceiving and testing supersonic aircraft, even down to the very tools that we used. There were several examples of this. For instance, the airflow over the P1's wings was very similar to Concorde's in that we depended on the profile of the leading edge to create the low pressure vortices above the wing. This pioneering work on the P1 was certainly instrumental in the success of the SST concept. There was also a direct link. I was delighted to discover an assembly shop full of Lightning tools, jigs and equipment at Filton because the forward fuselages of all 20 dual-seat Lightning T5s were built there by the same men who went on to build Concorde. Overall, a total of more than 330 Lightnings of various marks were produced.

The mathematical analyses required in the design of the P1B/Lightning and Concorde were surprisingly similar. Slide rules and mechanical adding machines were the order of the day. A device that could have worked out square roots accurately and quickly would have been worth its weight in weapons-grade plutonium. In those days it was an iterative process of guesswork until you got sufficiently close to the answer. Today's free calculators given away on key-rings in Christmas crackers would have saved us hundreds of thousands of pounds – a lot of money back then! Some of the unwitting, or perhaps instinctive, design features of the P1 came to be recognised in later years and given posh names, but they were already there in Teddy Petter's original concept. For instance, the area rule concept (constant cross-sectional frontal area along the length of the aircraft) later much vaunted by the Americans, was a feature of the layout along with a much more extreme wing sweep than that used in other contemporary fighter aircraft designs.

This high degree of sweep, 60 degrees at the leading edge and 52 degrees at the trailing edge with only a 5% thickness ratio, kept the wing well behind the main shock waves. It also effectively spread the frontal area of the aircraft along its length, thus conforming to the area rule principle. A brilliant feature of the aircraft's engineering was just how 'right' the detailed design was from the very start. There was the famous day when the wing was statically tested to the point of failure. The load level was increased from 50% to 75% and then up to 95% of the predicted failure point when alarming creaks and groans could be heard from the structure. Eventually the 100% load level was reached and five seconds later there was a loud bang when part of the wing structure failed. It was impressive that this complex and advanced wing, where load paths were extremely difficult to predict, had precisely reached its design target. Many years later I found myself using techniques that the P1 design team were applying every day to solve the problems of structural strength and failure. For example, by removing metal rather than adding it, the overall strength and flexibility of an aircraft structure could be increased. Over-strong components acted as stress raisers whilst components that were too flexible transmitted the load to stiffer areas. We found that by weakening the over-stiff parts to create uniform stiffness and flexibility this worked wonders for weight-saving and fatigue life.

The genius of the original architecture of the P1 was apparent from the fact that the major details of the layout were frozen as early as 1951. The Sapphire engines (later Avons) stacked and staggered to reduce frontal area, the wing planform mounted at shoulder height, the 5% thickness profile and the all-moving tail plane mounted low down on the fuselage to operate in clear air – all remained unchanged through to the final mark of Lightning. It is worth emphasising the ingenuity of the engine layout. The stacked and staggered arrangement gave 100% increase in power with only a 50% increase in frontal area – brilliant!

A further bonus of the P1/Lightning programme was the development of supersonic wind tunnels. Although small in cross section and powered by early centrifugal gas turbines, these wind tunnels could test aircraft profiles up to Mach 1.7 which was revolutionary in the early 1950s. From these wind tunnel tests another important P1/Lightning 'first' was established: the aircraft would be capable of supercruise – the ability to cruise at supersonic airspeeds without the use of after-burners, something that was vital to the range (and economics) of Concorde many years later.

Without the use of computers in the design phase, the ultimate accolade to the engineers' work was that, in flight, the aircraft performed and handled almost exactly as had been predicted. This probably had a lot to do with the point that, very unusually, the legendary English Electric test pilot Roland (Bee) Beamont was invited to be an integral part of the design team from day one. Beamont was the first English pilot to fly an aircraft through the sound barrier which he did in an F86 Sabre. The P1s and the Lightning flew smoothly through the transonic phase which made the whole idea of a future supersonic passenger aircraft entirely credible. Of course the performance of the Lightning was remarkable, as suggested later by a flippant comment from a service pilot: "I was fully in charge, then I let the brakes off!"

"Had a little trouble losing cockpit canopies, but I think we've mastered it."

The flight test programme for the P1A and P1B went smoothly apart from the embarrassing loss of a few canopies due to the aeroelastic deformation of the canopy rails. Fortunately this did not result in any injuries. The only major changes for the production Lightning were the altered air intake to accommodate the Ferranti Airpass radar, a raised pilot seat and a larger fin. The Lightning was born – and what an aircraft it was! Designed for just ten years of Royal Air Force service, it actually completed 28 years from 1960 to 1988 during which time the Lightning never fired a shot in anger, unlike just about every one of its predecessors and successors. Famously, the Lightning shot down just one aircraft – one of ours! A pilot had ejected from his termi-

Above: 56 Squadron F1A in Firebird colour scheme.

Left: Firebird five-ship, 56 Squadron aerobatic team.

Below: 74 Squadron detachment, Darwin, Australia, June 1964 (Dave Roome)

Top left: 111 Squadron F1As in line abreast.

Top right: Three F3s and a lone T5 of Lightning Training Flight (LTF) in echelon starboard.

Above: 19 Squadron F2 over Yorkshire.

Left: 56, 111, 19 and 92 Squadrons – a mixture of markings of the 1960s.

Top: "Don't forget your bone dome, sir!" Kiwi Perreaux of 111 Squadron.

Above: 56 Squadron Lightning flown by Flight Lieutenant Richard Pike approaching the refuelling basket of a Victor tanker over Mount Etna, Sicily.

Top: 23 Squadron F6 cross training with a USAF KC135 tanker.

Below: F3 of 29 Squadron and Victor K2 of 57 Squadron over the Alps.

Bottom: A Soviet Bear bomber in the northern skies. In the foreground, a Lightning F6 of 23 Squadron shadows the Russians.

Top left: 74 Squadron F3 from RAF Leuchars near Carnoustie Golf Course, 1964.

Top right: T4 from 226 OCU with 65 Squadron markings.

Middle left: 5 Squadron F6 over North Sea oil rigs.

Middle right: Lightning Training Flight F3.

Above: A neat vic of 19 Squadron F2As from Gütersloh.

Top: Line up of 74 Squadron FIAs with Firestreak missiles and 30mm cannon attached.

Above left: F1A of the Leuchars Target Facilities Flight.

Above right: 92 Squadron F2As, led by Wing Commander Ed Durham, Germany, 31 December 1976.

Left: 11 Squadron F6 on the centre hose of a VC10 tanker.

Top: Flight Lieutenant Simon Morris makes approach and landing in 92 Squadron F2A 'D' (XN791), early 1970s.

Above: 11 Squadron's T5 among the trees of Belgian Air Force base, Kleine Brogel.

Left: Heavyweight 56 Squadron F6 with 270 gal over-wing fuel tanks fitted.

Above: 92 Squadron F2A with 4 Squadron Harrier.

Left: Camouflage trials for 11 Squadron F6 and T5.

Below: 5 Squadron F6s with varying camouflage schemes.

nally ill Harrier which was flying towards a population centre so a Lightning was sent up to despatch the Harrier, a task duly achieved.

The Lightning was renowned for its ear-splitting and spectacular vertical climb at just about every air show at which the aircraft was demonstrated. I will always remember a fabulous 'Diamond Nine' display by 74 Squadron. The high speed, near silent approach with white water vapour shimmering over their wings was a beautiful sight to behold. Then came that overwhelming wall of sound as the Lightnings drew level, stood on their tails and seemed to climb into the heavens forever. The din should have woken the dead for 50 miles around and the emotional impact was palpable. Many moist eyes in the crowd were being wiped after that display.

This performance, though, was more than just a crowd pleaser – it was real. Whilst the Lightning could not maintain its astonishing initial rate of climb of 50,000 feet per minute, the aircraft could easily reach an altitude of 40,000 feet in 2.5 minutes and there are recorded instances of Lightnings, with missiles fitted, climbing to over 85,000 feet. This was the territory of the Lockheed U-2 high altitude reconnaissance aircraft with its 103-feet wingspan and must have caused considerable surprise and alarm to any United States U-2 pilot who found a British colleague grinning at him from alongside.

The Lightning has beaten the McDonnell Douglas F15 Eagle up to 30,000 feet and out-climbed many other later aircraft like the McDonnell Douglas F4 Phantom, the variable-sweep wing Grumman F14 Tomcat, the General Dynamics F16 Freedom Fighter, the Dassault Mirage III, the variable-sweep wing Panavia Tornado and last, but not least, the Mikoyan-Gurevich MiG-21 (NATO code-named 'Fishbed'). It has been said that the Lightning was the fastest pilot-only aeroplane ever built in that the machine lacked sophisticated on-board computers – the pilot had to do it all. Today's combat aircraft are designed to be inherently unstable with stability only achieved by two or three computers working in parallel to obey the pilot's instructions. If the computers fail most of these aircraft will become unflyable. The Lightning was the most manoeuvrable Mach 2 fighter of its generation. One of the trickier aspects about flying it, however, was landing in a crosswind at nearly 200 mph, the skinny tyres always making that a bit of a lottery, particularly on a wet runway.

The Lightning, because of its complexity and the packaging density of its systems, was difficult and highly labour-intensive to maintain. There's a worst case report of one thousand hours of maintenance required to achieve just one flying hour. Hopefully this was the exception rather than the rule. The Lightning story would not be complete without mentioning the rather grim statistic that crashes and other accidents accounted for more than a third of the aircraft built; for various reasons nearly 120 Lightnings were lost over its service life. The single major cause of loss was fire, both in the air and on the ground, which accounted for 33 aircraft. Undercarriage problems disposed of a further 18 aircraft, six were lost in mid-air collisions, two ran out of fuel and one aircraft somehow or other managed to ingest a display banner.

If money was no object it would be interesting to fit a Lightning with modern electronics and more fuel efficient engines. These measures would overcome the aircraft's two major deficiencies and the Lightning's performance could still embarrass most military aircraft flying today. Even the P1A, with its early engines, could top 1,000 mph, the P1B nearly 1,400 mph and the Lightning over 1,500 mph.

It may surprise people to learn that Concorde's potential as a supersonic bomber was the subject of a brief and classified study in the British Aircraft Corporation. This came to nothing because it soon became obvious that a few squadrons of Concorde would have consumed the entire defence budget twice over. The Polaris submarine-launched missile with its multiple re-entry warheads was a much more cost-effective deterrent. However, it amuses me to think that the one aeroplane which could have caught and destroyed a Concorde bomber was the Lightning, conceived when I, born in the Second World War, was just four years old. The Lightning was an astonishing aeroplane and a wonderful example of British engineering genius at its very best.

CHAPTER 12

IN FFOLIO-FFOSTER'S F-FOOTSTEPS

MICHAEL BETTELL IN A QUANDARY

I had not looked forward to the flight. As the squadron new-boy I was required to undergo a check-ride with my new boss, a complex individual whose reputation, not to mention his embarrassing habit of brawling in the officers' mess with the rival Lightning squadron's CO, was hardly confidence-boosting. During the pre-flight briefing, my mercurial CO had been to the point: no small talk, no easy chit-chat to pass the time of day, nothing frivolous to interfere with the job in hand. In the end, despite an air of tension, my check-ride in a Hunter T7 (no two-seater Lightning had been available) had gone reasonably well and it was on the next flight, my first in a single-seat Lightning Mark 3 on my new squadron –111(F) Squadron based at RAF Wattisham in Suffolk – that the problems began.

The initial part of this 'first solo' proved straightforward enough. After somewhat cautious start-up, taxy and take-off procedures, I climbed up to an altitude of around 36,000 feet, carried out some high level work, orientated myself with local navigational features, then informed the controller that I would return to Wattisham for some practice circuits. The year was 1966, the April weather was exemplary and I was having a fine old time in my brand new

Lightning Mark 3 with its innovative cockpit layout. As I flew towards the airfield, I had a strong sense of being at one with the world while I observed the Suffolk landscape, its medley of soft colours, the subtle contrasts within the coastal area to the east. Few hills or valleys were evident here, just a patchwork of flat fields with haphazard villages that gently poked and prodded their way into adjacent countryside. In time, I would grow to love this area which would become my home more or less ever since these early days. When not required for squadron duties, I would potter around on my Lambretta scooter while I explored picturesque surroundings that were markedly different from those of RAF Binbrook in Lincolnshire where, eight years previously as a thirteen-year-old cadet, I had sampled my first taste of the Royal Air Force.

Of course, I was young and wide-eyed back then, even so it was apparent at an early stage that this could be the life for me. I had loved the atmosphere, the barrack room banter, the whole scenario which seemed so much more fun than the plodding routines and heavy hassles of many civilian orbits. In the station NAAFI I could eat as much as I liked and I could drink gallons of pop to my heart's content. I even enjoyed the visit to a fish factory in nearby Grimsby. When it had come to my turn for an air experience flight, I could hardly contain my excitement. I'd been scheduled to fly in an Avro Anson, a relic of World War 2 but used subsequently as a communications aircraft, a navigational trainer, and as a general dogsbody machine. If the aeroplane lacked glamour, it was legendary nonetheless.

Our pilot was called Flight Lieutenant Ffolio-Ffoster (yes, he really was) and he had a large handlebar moustache (he really did). He talked of chatting-up popsies and wizard prangs, and he'd told us a story of how, in June 1940, that momentous stage when Prime Minister Churchill had declared that 'the Battle of France is over, the Battle of Britain is about to begin', a flight of three Ansons had been attacked by nine Luftwaffe Messerschmitt 109 fighters. Despite what must have seemed like a Sisyphean task, the Anson crews had fought back heroically and aggressively. In an astonishing turn of events, the Anson men had downed two German fighter aircraft and damaged a third before the dogfight ended. All three Ansons had survived the battle. Flight Lieutenant Ffolio-Ffoster had told us, too, of a sensational scrape in Australia where two Ansons, having collided in mid-air, became locked together. In spite of this, the pilots had made a successful emergency landing at Brocklesby, New South Wales after which one of the airframes was repaired and the machine flew again.

I'd naturally been awed by such dashing tales of adventure. When Ffolio-Ffoster and his Avro Anson had launched (or what is lurched?) from Binbrook to head for the coast, I'd been fascinated by the sights of the Lincolnshire countryside that stretched sublimely into the distance, scenes of green and purple against blue skies and scattered April cumulus. As we reached the coastline, Flight Lieutenant Ffolio-Ffoster descended to low level where he conducted a 'beat-up' of the open, sandy stretches of Skegness beach. I had not flown before – I had not even seen inside an aircraft – and the experience was overwhelming. That night, I dreamt about flying. When I awoke in the morning, I resolved there and then that I would try to become a pilot.

Not long after the Combined Cadet Force camp at Binbrook, I posted off my application to join the service under the Royal Air Force scholarship scheme. I was summonsed for assessment at the selection centre at RAF Hornchurch, and all had gone well for the initial phase. Regretfully, however, I was not accepted for a scholarship at the RAF College, Cranwell. In a state of considerable despondency, therefore, I left school at the age of sixteen to do what my mother had always wanted me to do: become an articled clerk to a firm of chartered accountants in London. For two years, rows of London houses and shops, curious back streets, interminable traffic, the Tube, the bus routes to the office, the office itself, my small desk in the office, formed the main horizon and track of my life, an insipid and circumscribed world. If, at that tender age, I had begun to learn harsh lessons, to think that my way of life was consigned inevitably to a certain conduit of accepted conditions, it was the bright lights of a Royal Air Force recruiting centre in Holborn, central London that suddenly raised my sights. Lit up like a colourful Christmas tree, the recruiting centre caught my eye as I sat in a taxi on my way back to the accountancy office after meeting a client. I ordered the taxi to stop, paid the driver and made my way into the recruiting centre.

As soon as I stepped inside that centre, memories of Avro Anson aircraft, of Skegness beach, of wizard prangs and chatting-up popsies, of Flight Lieutenant Ffolio-Ffoster with his handlebar moustache came flooding back. I walked over to the reception desk where a charming gentleman, a flight lieutenant with – wait for it – a magnificent handlebar moustache, greeted me like a long lost friend. Just because I had not been accepted for a scholarship at Cranwell, he explained, that did not mean I was excluded from an alternative scheme, a direct entry commission for which 'A' level examinations were not required. My current crop of 'O' levels were perfectly acceptable for the direct entry method. My God, I thought, why hadn't someone explained this before? I've wasted two years. Needless to say, I signed on the dotted line in double-quick time and it was not long before I presented myself to the authorities at RAF South

Cerney where I underwent four months of tough basic training.

Having passed the course at South Cerney, I entered the flying training system at the end of which – fantastic! – I was posted to the Lightning Operational Conversion course at RAF Coltishall. Coltishall, to me, was an eye-opener; probably the happiest station of my service career. For the first time I felt that the staff treated their students as adults. My first solo in a Lightning, a Mark F1, was an eye-opener, too. It was towards Christmas in 1964, the sun was low in the west and on final approach to landing I suddenly realised that I could not see properly: in their pre-flight inspection, the groundcrews had forgotten to clean the windshield; the combination of low sun and smeared perspex produced an opaque effect. Left floundering, I overshot from the approach and made a radio call to the duty instructor, Flight Lieutenant Graydon, for advice. "Try to look out of the side-windows," he said, "you should get a better perspective of the runway." The suggestion worked, and I managed to land safely.

Seemingly destined for problems on first solo flights, my first night solo at Coltishall was not trouble-free either. The start-up and take-off procedures worked out okay but once airborne, when I attempted to use my electrical seat-height adjustment system, the motor ran away and the seat became stuck in the fully-up position. As a fairly tall individual, this meant that my 'bone dome' (flying helmet) was pushed hard against the top of the canopy with my head cranked through ninety degrees. I may have felt – and looked – like a right humperdink but at the time the situation was far from amusing. There'd been little point in radioing for help this time so, in a state of considerable anxiety, I returned to the airfield and set myself up for a touchdown at around 155 knots (approximately 175 miles per hour). This high-speed hurtle into a black hole with runway lights around the ears was precarious enough at the best of times, however, fortunately the finals approach worked out that night and, fingers firmly crossed, I managed to pull off a successful landing.

Just now, as I flew across the Suffolk countryside towards Wattisham, I had a warm feeling of satisfaction. Since those dark days in London, life had turned out well for me; at long last I had achieved my aim. The heady ambition that had followed my thirteen-year-old aspirations as a cadet at Binbrook had materialised. I felt, in fact, that a small pat on the back would not go amiss at present. I spoke to the local air traffic controller at Wattisham, obtained clearance to join the airfield circuit and, once overhead, 'broke' hard towards the downwind leg. As part of the pre-landing checks, I selected the undercarriage down and glanced at the indicator. Normally three red lights would appear, followed fairly swiftly by three green lights. This would confirm that the undercarriage was down and locked. Nothing, though, appeared – no reds, no greens, nothing. With a prompt sense of disbelief, I stared at the indicator. In my inexperience, I had failed to note the familiar 'clunk' of undercarriage movement; it could have happened, but I was unsure. Suddenly, my state of pleasant reverie had turned to one of querulous quandary.

The Lightning Pilots' Notes were unequivocal on the subject of undercarriage problems: in the event of undercarriage failure, the Lightning should be abandoned because the aircraft was likely to cartwheel on landing. No ifs, no buts – just fly to a suitable area and eject. I asked the controller if he could see whether my undercarriage was down but, in a somewhat unhelpful reply, he declined to say one way or the other. It crossed my mind that his mega-huge, mega-powerful and no doubt mega-expensive binoculars could be put to good use at this moment, but I had no stomach for argument. "Is the duty pilot available?" I asked timidly.

"We're trying to find him," said the controller.

Meanwhile, I set up an orbit above the airfield while I waited for the duty pilot to arrive. I wondered whether I should attempt a further undercarriage selection, but decided this may not be a good idea. As I flew in circles above the airfield, I gazed gloomily at my Lightning's fuel guages. I began to calculate the amount of fuel required to climb to an altitude of around 10,000 feet while I headed towards the coast for a suitable ejection area. I would aim to point the Lightning out to sea before I pulled the ejection seat handle. I prompted the controller again: "any sign of the duty pilot yet?" but the reply was negative.

By this stage, with my fuel state close to the level I had calculated for the 'ejection' option, I was becoming seriously worried. There seemed little point in operating the undercarriage emergency lowering system, on the other hand I reckoned there was little to lose. I glanced down at the yellow and black painted handle positioned low in the cockpit. This handle, I noticed, was placed immediately, and inconveniently, next to another, also daubed in yellow and black. Still in a state of fluster, I reached for what I thought was the correct handle and tugged it upwards. At once, I was aware that I had mistakenly jettisoned the Lightning's fuel ventral tank. The tank, observed by the controller, apparently fluttered down like a leaf before landing harmlessly in a field.

At about this point the duty pilot's breathless voice called me on the aircraft radio. After a few terse exchanges, he confirmed that he could see that the undercarriage was down. "Turn downwind and land immediately," he instructed. With trepidation, I carried out the order and felt a surge of relief when the undercarriage system withstood the landing.

It did not take long for the engineers to establish that the fault had been a gauge error and that the undercarriage system itself was fully serviceable. A more experienced pilot would have been aware of the undercarriage 'clunk' when the wheels were lowered; a fair degree of pointless panic would have been avoided, as well as the lamentable loss of a fuel ventral tank.

I signed in the aircraft after landing, then awaited the inevitable summons to the boss's presence. This occurred quite quickly and as I made my way towards his office, a black cloud of doom seemed to form above my head. I tried to cheer myself up with thoughts of the evening when, with a squadron colleague no doubt, I would head for the officers' mess bar to drown a few sorrows. I imagined that tonight's conversation would be brusque, like the one I was about to have with the CO:

"Beer?"

"Yes, beer please."

"Cheers."

"Cheers!" We would lift our glasses and drink.

"Awful beer."

"Yes, awful beer."

"Bad day?"

"Yes, terrible…"

At about this point, I reached the CO's dreaded door. I hesitated for a moment or two before entering. I placed my hat on my head and tried to make sure that it was straight. When, eventually, I felt sufficiently prepared, I knocked timorously on the door. A bold voice from within commanded: "Come!"

I entered the room, closed the door behind me, then turned round as I came to attention smartly and saluted. The squadron leader had an earnest, energised air. His expression of rage seemed to be accompanied by strange snorting and sucking noises. A pilot of renowned ability, he was a large, good-looking man with a dark, open face which did not hide anything. His eyes, bright and dark, were rarely still unless staring into your own. His hair was black and swept back.

"Well?" he said.

As I attempted to launch into defensive explanations, he raised one hand to demand silence. He then began a vehement one-way conversation at the end of which I was offered no chance to reply. After a few moments of awkward silence, he raised one hand again in a small gesture of anguish then let it drop by his side. "You're grounded," he said.

And so it was: grounded for a period, as well as two weeks of dreary orderly officer duties. Looking back, this punishment was inappropriate and unduly harsh. However, I was young, impressionable, ingenuous. Furthermore, I felt disinclined to pick a fight with a dragon, especially one who was experienced in the art of bar brawling. Later, I had other opportunities when the CO's undoubted talents encouraged my progress on the squadron. At the time, though, I took the punishment on the chin and with the positive thought that it was better, at least, than two years spent as an articled clerk to a firm of accountants in London.

CHAPTER 13

BEAR REACTION

Five-ship formation of 5(F) Squadron Lightnings.

ALAN WINKLES ON THE BRINK

The female controller's nervous tone added to my own sense of apprehension. No doubt the circumstances of my scramble had intensified our mutual, if unspoken, anxiety. She handled the intercept geometry well, though, and her logical instructions meant that I was in a good position to identify the Soviet machines when I rolled out behind them. At that stage, however, matters were relatively straightforward; the dilemmas were yet to come.

Several months had gone by since my last quick reaction alert scramble but that was not so unusual; as a member of 5(F) Squadron based at Binbrook in Lincolnshire, I was used to our somewhat backwater location. The lion's share of QRA activity was handled by our colleagues at RAF Leuchars in Scotland and, to be truthful, I would feel envious of their tales of action, excitement and general derring-do that would filter down after Soviet aircraft interceptions.

By mid-September 1968, with my squadron's lack of involvement in QRA activity, it was, perhaps, understandable if a certain lethargy afflicted those on QRA duty for a 24-hour stint. The rush of adrenaline, therefore, was probably all the greater when word was received one day from the controller at Patrington, a ground radar unit near Hull, that Soviet 'zombies' identified by the Royal Norwegian Air Force were headed our way. More often than not these so-called zombies would turn out to be Bear D (Tupolev Tu-95 RT) aircraft en route to Castro's communist Cuba via the Iceland/Faroes gap. Matters, though, were different on this day – Wednesday, 18th September 1968 – and, as events progressed, the situation became increasingly tense. We were armed with live weapons and the use of armed intervention on that day seemed to come perilously close.

To keep us up-to-date with the overall scenario, the Patrington controller used his direct 'telebrief' link to our QRA set-up. We learnt that the zombies had flown past Bergen on the Norwegian coast and were headed for Denmark. We learnt, too, that instead of the usual pair of Bear Ds there appeared to be large formations of aircraft. As a consequence, alarm bells were set off across NATO as military forces came to higher states of readiness. It must have been around mid-day when I was brought to cockpit readiness and given scramble instructions. I was ordered to head for a point about 100 miles east of Great Yarmouth in Norfolk where I was required to hold a combat air patrol (CAP). I would fly neat patterns in the sky until needed by the master controller at Neatishead, Suffolk while he monitored the 'big picture'.

As the first fighter to reach the CAP area, I was on my own initially. Flying at the Lightning's most fuel-efficient airspeed I held a two-minute race-track pattern at 36,000 feet. From time to time the controller announced: "no trade at present". His tone, somewhat lacklustre, inferred that he expected the zombies to turn around and head back home soon. If that happened, in turn I would have to fly back to my own base. Anticipating such an instruction, I could not avoid a sense of disappointment; how great it would have been if, just for once, I could have experienced a small slice of the action so regularly enjoyed by the Leuchars wing.

If I had begun to feel sorry for myself, however, such feelings had to be swiftly set aside when the controller next spoke. "The zombies have turned away from the Danish coast," he said. "They're now heading 270 degrees."

"Zombies heading 270?"'My voice may have gone up in tone when I asked this.

"Affirmative," said the controller, whose own voice had assumed a sudden urgency. "Looks like a dozen zombies are heading this way."

"Acknowledged," I said. A dozen! Bloody hell!

"Maintain your CAP for now," said the controller.

"Copied," I said. Where's everyone else? I thought. I've got twelve zombies, two missiles and zero back-up. Blimey!

"Standby," said the controller. "Turn onto an easterly heading now and increase your airspeed to Mach 0.9."

"Roger," I said and as I turned, I stared due east momentarily before concentrating on my AI 23B radar cockpit indicator. With my left thumb I carefully rotated a knob on the hand controller to adjust the radar's scanner angle. I used another switch to modify the scanner's 'search' mode (with over a dozen separate switches on the hand controller, the truism 'one-armed paper hanger' was apposite when applied to Lightning pilots). Meanwhile, the Neatishead controller instructed me to change to a different radio frequency and to check in with another controller. The radar unit, it appeared, had summoned more staff urgently to deal with the developing situation. The new controller's anxious female voice reflected the seriousness of what was going on around us. Despite this, clearly she had been well trained and her instructions were coherent and rational as she set up a 180-degree intercept geometry (the fighter, in this case, would turn through 180 degrees when adjacent to the target to roll out half-a-mile or so behind).

"Targets' range 100 miles," she said, at which I selected the longest range scale on my AI 23B.

"Descend now to 32,000 feet."

"Descending." I eased back the Rolls-Royce Avon's twin throttles.

"Maintain Mach 0.9," she said.

"Copied," I said. My current throttle setting would maintain the required airspeed in the descent.

"Turn twenty degrees to the port for displacement."

"Acknowledged." I eased the Lightning leftwards and made a mental note that my final turn onto targets' heading would now be to the right.

"Targets' range down to 80 miles," she said.

"80 miles." I continued to press my forehead against the rubber shade as I squinted anxiously at the two-and-a-half inch screen of my cockpit radar indicator.

"Confirm your altitude," she said.

"I'm just approaching 32,000 feet."

"Okay. Maintain that height." I glanced up briefly to try to spot the incoming masses, but I saw nothing yet. I looked down for a moment to observe vast undulating stretches of cloud formed above the North Sea. As I returned my gaze to the radar picture the controller said: "The targets' range is now reducing to 55 miles and they're slightly above your present altitude."

I acknowledged her call and made a minor adjustment on my hand controller. It was at this point that my heart must have missed a beat and a sliver of ice seemed to shoot its way into my intestines. The first 'paints' on my radar screen were followed by others until, like green goblins on the rampage, the screen swiftly became swamped. As if an airborne tsunami approached, grim communist hordes were represented by the green 'paints' on my tiny radar screen. The formations seemed ubiquitous and relentless. By now, maybe, the incoming crews had spotted their sole contestant on their own radars; my minority-of-one presence must have appeared absurd – risible – as they prepared to pounce. Absurd or not, I was committed to the defence of my mother country and any sense of loneliness had to be put to the back of my mind as I concentrated on my radar screen.

"Contact with the targets," I said to the controller, "keep talking." Normally I would have taken control of the intercept at this stage but under the circumstances I opted for 'close control'.

Although the nervous edge to her voice remained, the controller continued to give good directions. Before long, a glance at the sky confirmed what she and my radar were telling me: this tsunami was no mere figment of the imagination. Radar blips had transmuted into massive machines with great red stars painted on the sides. I was staring at the carriers of nuclear weapons, symbols of dystopia, devils bent on death and destruction on an abominable scale.

"Standby to turn onto the targets' heading," said the controller. As if I was sat in a dentist's chair anticipating a malevolent practitioner about to lunge, I waited anxiously for the crunch moment. Her crucial words eventually came: "Now turn starboard through 180 degrees," she cried.

I applied 60 degrees angle of bank and kept my eyes firmly out of the Lightning's cockpit as I turned towards the selected zombie, the second in the lead formation. This turn proved to be less than straightforward. As I became progressively mixed-up with miscellaneous sections of the Soviet Long Range Bomber Force, I had to ease my angle of bank every few seconds to check that the area was clear of possible collision risk. The situation was not helped by prodigious contrails which criss-crossed the sky like scenes from WW2 black-and-white movies of RAF Bomber Command raids. At times it felt as if the day was darkening into night; my active imagination started to visualise vengeful footsteps that crept along like the feet of pursuit in a bad dream.

By the conclusion of my jerky turn through 180 degrees, I managed to stabilise the Lightning's position on the left side of the chosen zombie. This machine turned out to be a Bear B – the bomber version of the Bear fleet – and I closed slowly to a position about 100 yards abeam. I noted the tail number, markings, crew reaction, camouflage and other significant features then advanced the Lightning's throttles to overtake. I aimed now for the Bear ahead which, with its large radar dome underneath, proved to be the Bear D maritime surveillance version. As I pulled alongside I became aware of radio chatter from Neatishead: Lightning Mk 3s from RAF Wattisham had been scrambled together with Victor tanker air-to-air refuelling support. This was hardly the heavy brigade compared to my current neighbourhood, nonetheless the prospect of support boosted my morale. Another problem, though, had begun to dominate my thought processes: the Norfolk coast was looming.

The boundary between international and United Kingdom airspace, set at twelve miles from the coast, was a line of sacrosanct significance – violation by a potential enemy would shoot the heebie-jeebies at Hurricane Force 12 through the corridors of power up to the highest levels of government. One option was for me to fly alongside and just forward of the captain's cabin on the left side, waggle my wings, then commence a slow turn to the left to indicate that the intercepted aircraft should follow. This was an internationally agreed signal but such an option looked a little unrealistic (to put it politely) in current circumstances. My other choice was less palatable: to arm my air-to-air missiles in preparation for an order to fire. The mathematics now became interesting. The infrared heat seekers of my Red Top missiles needed two minutes to warm up. We were flying at eight miles a minute. I therefore needed to select missile cooling by at least 28 miles from the coast. My present range from the coast was 35 miles.

"Request permission to arm up," I asked the young controller. A horrible pause ensued until her voice, now markedly shrill, replied somewhat ambiguously: "Standby."

As the miles ticked by I could almost hear arguments raging in the background. I wondered idly how far up the line the issue would travel. At what point would Mr Dennis Healey, the Secretary of State for Defence, be contacted? Perhaps he was in his office, or maybe having an afternoon nap, or possibly enjoying lunch with Prime Minister Harold Wilson – which would be handy from the decision-making point of view, though far be it for me, I reckoned considerately, to cause them to choke on their beer and sandwiches. Maybe they were already in worried debate about last month's Soviet invasion of Czechoslovakia. Perhaps this would influence their earnest discussions in the urgent decision now needed.

At a range of 30 miles from the coast I repeated my request to arm up. The controller's reply, the same as last time, left me on tenterhooks. With just two miles to go to the calculated critical point I needed a decision fast. The decision, regretfully, was not forthcoming by the time I flew past the 28-mile point and my situation felt increasingly invidious. At 25 miles, still lacking any form of guidance, I resolved to make my own decision. Operation of the missile coolant switch, a procedure detectable by groundcrews, might lead to awkward questions. Nevertheless, I reached down and selected the coolant on. In two minutes' time, if and when an order to fire was given, all I had to do was to obtain a radar lock-on and ensure that the relevant missile switch was selected. A small squeeze on the trigger by one finger on my right hand and...Bingo!...the Soviet Long Range Bomber Force would be minus one Bear. The process could be rapidly repeated after which they would be minus two Bears. I preferred not to think of the six or seven-man crew ensconced inside each aircraft. I preferred, too, not to dwell on the reaction of the other members of the Soviet force.

As the Norfolk coast came into view, and with the range still counting down relentlessly, Neatishead continued to remain ominously quiet. Something must be done, I thought, this cannot be allowed to go on. If seismic stirrings behind the scenes had created alarm and despondency, that was just too bad. I was the one faced with the here-and-now; if the 'system' could not, or would not, offer suitable support then I would have to act on my own initiative. The system had failed me, full stop. In this parlous twilight zone of endless vacillation, someone, somewhere needed to show a bit of grit. If that someone had to be me and if, for the sake of the country – the world, even – a real-life James Bond in the form of me was needed, then so be it.

If such musings seem somewhat inflated, try to place yourself in my situation. The moment was pivotal; the stakes could hardly have been higher. To put things in perspective, just imagine, for instance, the elementary yet dire precautions that had to be made by households in WW2 – buildings sandbagged, wired, guarded, shuttered-up; gardens left untended and cluttered with the dreary accoutrements of war; guns and gun carriages, tents, trucks, gas-caped soldiers, like swarms of giant green insects, that occupied streets, farms, woods, fine countryside which had become shabby, neglected, only half-alive; concrete pill-boxes, some covered in paint, others in domestic disguise to resemble post offices, shops, hay-stacks, vehicles as the populace struggled with crude camouflage to thwart bomb-aimers...just imagine how such efforts would need to be doubled and re-doubled in a nuclear scenario. Even then, the activities could turn out to be futile. Now imagine the responsibility felt by a sole pilot, a young man in his early twenties, whose duty it was to forestall such cataclysmic prospects.

At a range of fifteen miles from the coast, I began to advance my throttles. My Red Top missiles remained on full 'red alert' but I had no intention of firing them without authority. Left with no other choice, I was therefore determined to try the 'follow me' tactic. At twelve miles from the coast, as I drew level with the Bear D's cockpit, I attempted to stare in the captain's direction. The cockpit windows were small, however, and I was uncertain of the captain's reaction. At ten miles from the coast, just as I was about to take up the internationally recognised 'follow me' position, the great Bear D suddenly dipped its starboard wing as the captain initiated a turn due north.

If I had time to breathe a sigh of relief, it was surely a deep one. As I followed the lead Bear D's turn, a glance over my right shoulder revealed a remarkable sight. An eccentric mix of Bears, Lightnings, Victor tanker aircraft trailed behind in a spontaneously-formed, unofficial formation. Multiple contrails added to the curious spectacle which had begun to assume positively surreal proportions. As the incongruous convoy weaved its way northwards, it was in the vicinity of Flamborough Head that I handed over 'my' pair of Bears to Lightnings from the Leuchars wing. I then turned away hard and set my heading for Binbrook.

Later, we learnt that the cause of the day's furore had been a 'graduation' flight by the Bear operational conversion unit based near Murmansk. Evidently the instructors there had wanted to take their students on a different route to normal.

As for me, the effect of the day's experience had been profound. The system had been found wanting; lessons needed to be learned at many different levels. Like a key pawn in a grand game of chess, great decisions had been left largely in my own hands and the intense concentration required had left me with a feeling of deep fatigue. I endured disturbed dreams that night.

CHAPTER 14

EYES TIGHT SHUT

SIMON MORRIS IN SORE NEED

The presence of mountains did not help one bit. Just last night, as dusk fell, I had watched those mountains and observed strange streaks of light across the sky where the sun had gone down behind clouds. As I stood there, drinking in the atmosphere, miscellaneous aromas – orange blossom, smoke, silage – had filled the air. This was an unusual spot, I'd thought, but a fine one even so; a place with a good feeling about it, although that did not exactly help my problem.

"Just to let you know that I got back safely," I said when I rang my girlfriend. The telephone line had been crackly but more or less usable.

"Sure you'll be all right?" she asked

"Yes...no..." I vacillated

"Don't leave it too long...*mañana*...and all that," she said.

"I'm not in Spain," I said.

"Where are you then?"

"I'm in Sardinia."

"Oh yes," she said. "Lucky break. What language do they speak there?"

"Bugger knows."

"What?" she said.

"I meant, good question."

"You're in a fix, then," she said.

"Tell me about it."

In spite of everything, I'd perked up after the conversation. It had seemed like a knockabout farce at times but at least it hadn't developed into a knock-about disaster. You're not yourself, I'd thought, but then I was suffering – and not just from an over-indulgence of Chianti.

The next day, as the sun rose, I was driven with colleagues to the airfield operations set-up for meteorological and other briefings. I was a member of 92(F) Squadron based at Gütersloh in Germany and now part of a detachment of squadron personnel sent to the Italian air force base at Decimomannu (which in Latin, so we were told, meant 'ten miles from Cagliara') in the southern reaches of Sardinia. During the five-week detachment we would make use of the weapons range to the west of Sardinia to fire Aden cannon fitted in the nose sections of our Mark F2A Lightnings. We would aim at a towed target – a long white flag attached behind an English Electric Canberra crewed by brave souls.

There was an air of excitement as we bumped along in the aircrew bus. By

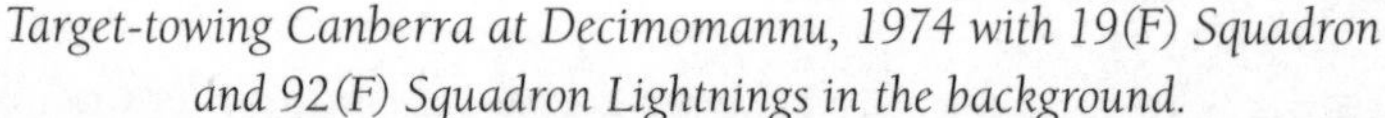

Target-towing Canberra at Decimomannu, 1974 with 19(F) Squadron and 92(F) Squadron Lightnings in the background.

Simon Morris in the near Lightning (aircraft 'F'), Ali McKay is his number two. Note that aircraft 'F' was low on fuel therefore one engine had been shut down hence the higher angle of attack.

the perimeter fence were lines of tranquil trees, a curious contrast to hectic airfield activity. The landscape beyond, an incongruous mix of olive trees, cork trees, scrub, rocky terrain, was populated by folk in remote villages with modest pseudo-Byzantine villas. To the west lay the Sulcis mountain range with Monte Linas rising to some 3,500 feet. Occasionally, when not required for flying, some of us would explore the area on foot. Just now, as I stared out from the grubby windows of the aircrew bus, I could imagine the plangent tones of bells of goats and other animals roaming the foothills. To the west, a light sea breeze would wander in and out, and rustle the olive leaves so that each one flashed a tangled semaphore of dark green and silver. *Ficus Carica*, the Sardinian fig, best eaten straight from the tree, seemed set apart, oddly aloof. Less aesthetic were poppies and other wild flowers which would sway amid rough grasses seared by the heat of summer. Sardinian warbler birds would flit and squabble while hedgehogs snuffled beneath them, rooting around to provide providential nests of grass and leaves.

I pondered the contrast between nature's prowess and the fiasco of war in these parts – or more to the point, the fiasco of Mussolini's war. To the north and west of Decimomannu was a village built by the fascist government in the 1920s. Now called Arborea, the village was originally named Villagio Mussolini before being upgraded to the debatedly catchier Mussolinia di Sardegna. En route to the firing range, our transit flights would take us near Iglisias, a village where violent fascist blackshirts had held meetings in the early 1920s.

These matters, of course, were ancient history – an ignoble past. Now it was July 1974, the Italians were on our side...although some, apparently, didn't always see things that way. "For ze next war," a German controller back at Gütersloh had remarked one time, "it is *your* turn to have ze Italians." The Germans, it appeared, still harboured bitter feelings towards their one-time ally. This became apparent at Decimomannu during conversations in messes. Along with our squadron detachment was a Luftwaffe squadron equipped with F104 Starfighters. "These people," a Luftwaffe officer said to me in hushed tones one evening in the officers' mess, "these Vops..." the German tongue never quite coped with the British term 'Wop' for Italians, "are *schrecklich* – terrible – *nicht*? In ze last war you came first and we were second. Those bloody Vops, though...they were ze great big third." Another time, I was in our operations room when we were contacted by the Luftwaffe squadron's duty officer. "A Vop has just crashed in the range," he said, "*nicht gut*. As a mark of respect we vill not permit any take-offs..." a slight sneer seemed sadly evident when he continued: "...for five minutes."

Despite all of this, nowadays the members of the Italian air force seemed efficient, the set-up at Decimomannu providing an effective facility used by many of NATO's air forces.

Before long, when the bus drew up at the operations centre, we disembarked to make our way to the briefing room. In the background we heard the enthusiastic tremolo of a would-be opera tenor practising his scales; I glanced at a fellow pilot who shrugged as if to say: 'we *are*, after all, surrounded by Italians, are we not?'

Our contingent of pilots now walked along corridors before filing into the briefing room where we sat down to listen, first of all, to the Italian weather man. This character, with his accented English and sleeveless jersey, droned on and on as seemed to be the habit of quite a few weather men. He discussed the menace of the Mistral winds, pointed a finger at swirly charts, meteorological models, convoluted analysis of this and that which amounted to a scientific synopsis of a good day with nice weather. The range officer spoke next. On a local aviation map he highlighted the range boundaries, talked about safety issues and explained current regulations. Take-off slots for range users, we were told, were rationed to a ratio of 70% for the Italians, 20% for the Germans and 10% for the Brits. I cogitated the reasons for this discrepancy – inversely proportional, so it seemed, to the 'results of ze last war', but such speculation did not get me very far.

On conclusion of the main briefing, we stood up to leave for the squadron's allocated building where we would conduct our own squadron briefings. As I was scheduled to lead a pair of Lightnings for the range sortie, I had to brief my fellow Lightning pilot on our specific procedures. The Lightning provided a stable platform for cannon firing, especially if just two cannons were employed; the concurrent use of all four cannons tended to induce excessive airframe vibration. We discussed this and other matters before gathering up our bone domes and Mae West lifejackets ready for the 'off'. Soon, having signed for our Lightnings, we performed external checks then clambered into cockpits for start-up and take-off procedures.

Quickly underway, we now flew towards the range. Sound airmanship dictated the need for a good 'lookout' – heads, in other words, had to remain firmly out of the 'office'. Occasional glances down to check cockpit instruments would last no more than a second or two, sufficient time, even so, to record like a camera the engines' oil pressures and temperatures, the aircraft fuel state, the oxygen reserves, the airspeed, the altitude and a dozen other items before, from force of habit, we resumed our search of the skies.

The transit flight did not take long and soon, having checked in on the aircraft radio with the range officer, it was time for proceedings to begin. At the pre-briefed height, I scrutinised the white flag that trailed behind the English Electric Canberra. The Canberra itself, daubed in 'Dayglo' red paint, held a steady heading. The sun was bright and from certain angles the white flag and the Canberra, Dayglo or not, were difficult to see. In turn, I peered anxiously at the flag, at my flight instruments, at the area ahead. From a 'perch' position above and to one side of the flag, I needed to judge the correct moment to commence the attack profile. I had to fly an accurate airspeed, height and heading: this was key – precise flying meant the difference between a good or bad result, success or failure. I felt keenly worried about failure – of letting down my squadron colleagues. Such thoughts caused my mind to churn and my throat to feel dry. Time, though, was short and, anxious or not, action was required.

At what I reckoned to be the right instant, I applied a high angle of bank. Simultaneously, I initiated a descent towards the target. Events happened fast. In a blur of weaves, turns, dives, pulls, speed adjustments and range assessments, the white flag hurtled towards me in no time at all.

Later, I would ruminate on the disparity between these controlled conditions and those faced by the Battle of Britain pilots. The contrast could hardly have seemed greater: we were well trained, well briefed and operated in a well regulated environment. The Hurricane and Spitfire pilots of 1940, on the other hand, had been hastily trained to be thrown into a scenario of merciless, messy combat – a mind-boggling hiatus, a desperate, dog-eat-dog affair where luck, as much as anything else, could prove crucial as a pilot struggled to close onto an enemy machine.

At present, however, such musings were not on my mind as I focussed on the job in hand. I squinted determinedly through my gunsight. The gunsight's cross had to be placed in the central area of the white flag. With harmonisation between the Aden 30mm cannon and the gunsight set at 300 yards, I counted down the range...900 yards...700 yards...500...400. At just over 300 yards, still closing fast, I used my right forefinger to squeeze the trigger on the control column. At once, I was aware of a crashing sound and sudden airframe vibration as the Aden cannon spat 'ball' ammunition at the target. In hostile operations the 'ball' ammunition would be replaced by high explosive rounds; just one round would be sufficient to down an enemy machine. My trigger squeeze did not last long – a mere half second or so. Then I applied a steep angle of bank to break away hard to avoid collision with the flag.

As swiftly as possible, I turned to reposition on the perch. Meantime, the other Lightning initiated his run against the flag. So it was that, in sequence, the two Lightnings spent some thirty minutes of target practice before another pair of Lightnings took over. At the end of the session, the Canberra would fly the white flag back to Decimomannu for inspection. With each pilots' ammunition dipped into different-coloured dyes, individual scores could be counted up. These scores, a disappointing three to four percent at first, were progressing gradually towards a more satisfactory 20 percent level as our skills improved and as the armourers tweaked the harmonisation between gunsight and cannon.

Just now, at the conclusion of the allotted 30-minute slot, I called the range officer to say that we intended to return to base. As I banked towards Decimomannu and began a climb to some 5,000 feet, I searched ahead for the 3,500 feet summit of Monte Linas – a distinctive navigational aid. The other Lightning quickly took up a loose formation position to the starboard side of my aircraft and at the designated point we both changed radio frequency to 'Roma Control'. It was shortly after this, subsequent to our check-in with the new controller and as we were about to cross the Sardinian coastline, that trauma struck. As if hit by a bullet destined for that recalcitrant white flag, I felt a sudden stab of pain in one tooth. I had experienced trouble with this molar before – the occasional twinge – and shortly before the squadron's departure to Decimomannu, I'd received temporary treatment...evidently a little too temporary. On the phone to my girlfriend the previous night I'd discussed the potential problems, but I'd not anticipated anything like this.

As best I could, I fiddled with my oxygen mask, attempted to wobble the tooth into some sort of submission, struggling to manipulate the jaw as one does. But it was no good: the torment persisted; the dreaded toothache showed no signs of receding. I therefore informed the other Lightning pilot of my problem and instructed him to speak with Roma Control. Then, without delay, I descended towards an adjacent valley: by flying as low as possible I hoped to ease the pressure differential which, no doubt, was exacerbating the toothache.

As I dived down, and despite my state of preoccupation, I picked up my colleague's conversation with Roma Control:

"The other Lightning has descended to low level," he said.

"Descended? Why? 'as he crashed?"

"No, no, he hasn't crashed."

"Where he crash?"

"He has *not* crashed."

"Why he crash?"

"I repeat...he has *not* crashed."

"What he doing then?"

"He's descended to low level."

A pause before the controller went on: "Why he descend?"

"If you must know," my colleague sighed. "He has toothache."

Another pause. "Toothache? What is this?" The controller appeared to be floundering. "Wait one," he said.

A further pause during which, from time to time, the controller's microphone appeared to become live. We heard the intermittent rustle of pages being turned and the odd guffaw in the background. When this developed into more obvious shrieks of jovial cackling, I realised that the controller and his colleagues must have consulted an Italian/English dictionary. At last, it seemed, they understood my problem. It might have been a good joke to them, I mused, but personally I felt in no mood at all for laughter.

Meantime, back at base, the squadron operations officer had been informed about my difficulty. Decimomannu soon came into view and I followed my colleague into the local airfield circuit. Before long, after I had landed my Lightning and signed the technical and operations logs, the operations officer sidled up to me. "Good man," he said cheerily, "I heard that you managed not to crash."

"A-hah," I said, for the lack of any intelligent remark that came immediately to mind.

"This surely bodes well for the future of mankind," he said.

I gave him a sideways look. "A-hah," I said with a frown designed to indicate disinterest in conversation let alone tiresome wisecracks.

"Your chariot is ready," he said as he pointed at the aircrew bus that was waiting to whisk me off to the base medical centre for emergency dental treatment.

Once there, it did not take me long to deduce that the Italian dentist could speak no English – not a word. No English, I thought, not a word? Ridiculous! What's wrong with the fellow? No wonder you came a great big third; my Luftwaffe friend was correct: these Vops were *schrecklich* all right. The dentist stared at me. He appeared to fix me with small wicked eyes and his expression suggested: 'we'll soon have you sorted, sunshine. Just try to relax, ho, ho.' His dental drill then headed south towards my open mouth. Meanwhile, I had my eyes tight shut.

CHAPTER 15

GOOD SHOOTING?

MARCUS WILLS AT MISSILE PRACTICE CAMP

As it rose in the east, I squinted anxiously at the sun now about the width of a man's hand above the horizon. Below, autumnal breezes swept across sand dunes, sped over taxiways and airfield paraphernalia, then hastened towards fields and distant hills; the whole countryside appeared in a state of windswept fluster as if in worried anticipation of winter. Like a lonely pariah set apart from the mainland of North Wales, the island of Anglesey's flat expanse, a curious contrast to the corrugations of high ground beyond the Menai Straits, extended to the Royal Air Force station at Valley in the western reaches of the island where, one day in mid-October 1967, I sat restlessly in my Lightning cockpit. I cast another hasty glance at my watch. The timing for our missile practice camp exercises was tight; I had to count down the minutes accurately before engine start: too early, and we could become short of fuel; too late, and we might miss our planned slot on the firing range.

I looked across at the Lightning parked next to mine, its canopy raised, its allotted groundcrews standing nearby. All seemed on tenterhooks. This was our last day at Valley before the 111 (F) Squadron personnel would conclude their detachment and return home to RAF Wattisham in Suffolk. It was a defining moment and we all felt the pressures. Of the detachment's allocation of Firestreak missiles, two were yet to be used and it was up to us to do our best to ensure a successful outcome. If we failed, a valuable training opportunity would be lost; missiles earmarked for practice firings were rationed strictly.

I gave a reassuring nod to my fellow Lightning pilot, Flight Lieutenant Dave

F/O Mullan, F/O Ellender, F/O Wills, S/L St. Aubyn, W/C Biddie, Capt Hall, F/O Allison, F/O Pike, F/O Mace and F/LT Sneddon at RAF Coltishall.

Hampton, who awaited my signal to start engines. He would act as my wingman for this flight. His face was hidden behind his oxygen mask, nonetheless I could picture his mischievous grin, his fingers drumming impatiently on the cockpit coaming. Despite the pressures, however, I knew that his talents as a pilot, his bubbly character and his infectious sense of humour would remain sound. A good friend of mine as well as a squadron colleague, I knew him well. In the officers' mess the previous night he had performed one of his favourite tricks: he would pick, slyly, an innocent-looking candidate sitting in a comfortable mess chair and who was about to enjoy a sip of hot coffee. I'd been in just such a situation last evening when he'd wandered up to me in a loose-jointed, amiable sort of way while he clutched his own cup of coffee. He'd said something like..."Ah, Marcus..." a jaunty little line, "did you hear that amazing news about…" at which point he'd pretended to trip up on the carpet, tipped his supposedly-full but actually-empty coffee cup, and aimed it directly at my lap. The shock of surprise, of course, had meant that some of my own coffee had slopped over me as I'd tried to twist clear. We'd exchanged glaring looks for a second, then the laughter had erupted. It had seemed the most comical thing that had ever happened. Accompanied by the guffaws and general merriment of others in the vicinity he'd said: "How careless of me!"

"Yes, very," I'd said.

"Slippery little critters these Welsh coffee cups," he'd gushed.

"Goes with the prevalent stink of disinfectant in this officers' mess, I suppose."

"Disinfectant? What's that?"

"Try that trick again and you're liable to find out!" More guffaws and banter had ensued.

I looked again at the waiting groundcrews. One man walked a few paces, shuffled round and glanced up at the sky before he stared at the Lightning cockpit as if willing us to start engines. Spread beside us were fire extinguishers, Houchin ground power units, wheel chocks and other miscellaneous equipment. The restive crewman checked his watch then shrugged his shoulders as if to say: 'time to start yet?' I shook my head in a negative motion. We'd have to be patient for a few more minutes yet.

I thought back to my training days, some of which had been spent here at Valley flying the Folland Gnat. However, my enthusiasm for aircraft and flying had developed long before that, probably back to the 1950s when my father would take me as a boy to Farnborough Air Shows, in those days held annually. With awe I would watch the likes of the Bristol Britannia, the de Havilland Comet, the Vickers Vanguard, the amazing Rolls-Royce-engined 'Flying Bedstead' and the Bristol Brabazon. The Brabazon, even by today's standards, was enormous. Powered by eight 'paired' Bristol Centaurus radial engines, the eccentric Brabazon's wingspan was 230 feet – some sixty feet greater even than the modern Boeing 767 400ER. Impossibly impractical, the only Brabazon ever built was scrapped in 1953. A few years later, I was intrigued by a story told by Bill Pegg, the Bristol Aeroplane Company's chief test pilot and a friend of my father. Mr Pegg told me how, for the Brabazon's first flight, uncertainty had surrounded the calculated airspeed at which the machine should become airborne. It was as if the Bristol Aeroplane Company had been resigned to doing what the British did best – just muddle through. When he'd taxied the Brabazon towards Filton's runway, Pegg had asked for clearance to enter the airfield's active runway.

"Do you intend to take off?" the Filton air traffic controller had asked.

"Dunno," Pegg had replied. "Wait and see!"

I was seventeen years of age when my father had taken me to Banwell in Somerset to meet Bill Pegg at his home. "So you want to be a pilot do you?" the great man had asked me.

"Indeed, sir."

"In that case I recommend that you do two things."

"Sir?"

"Firstly, you must read my book."

"I've read it already."

"Secondly, you must join the Royal Air Force."

Not long after that meeting I was able to tell Mr Pegg that I had been lucky enough to be selected for a scholarship at the RAF College at Cranwell in Lincolnshire. It was a heady time of my life and I could recall my first day at Cranwell clearly. When a somewhat rag-bag group of individuals were collected from Sleaford railway station by an air force bus, there'd been an air of appeal in all of our eyes as we'd gazed at each other in bewildered fashion. Then someone had said something amusing and I remember that everyone had laughed and all of our expressions had relaxed. Many years later we would understand the truism that friendships formed early in life tended to last the longest.

As new recruits, we were taken more or less directly to the camp barber after which we'd started a relentless round of slave labour to polish linoleum floors, bull-up brass taps and clean exposed water pipes in the flimsy wooden huts provided as accommodation by the Royal Air Force. We were hustled here and there by in-your-face sergeants, pestered with questions by members of the senior entry, given tasks that seemed to have little to do with military duties, let alone flying aeroplanes. We became immersed in unreality which, before too long, we accepted as eccentric but necessary. Today, our treatment back then would be regarded as outrageous bullying and would be outlawed, no doubt. At the time, though, a huge and intransigent common sense had been the secret of survival. We'd learned deep and thorough lessons which for most of us would provide invaluable tools for life.

The course at Cranwell had lasted for three years. After one year, the pilots and navigators had commenced their flying training. My flying instructor had seemed a rather humourless individual at first, though in time I'd learnt that behind his stern facade lay a keen, if dry, sense of humour. Towards the end of the course we had discussed posting choices. "What would be your preference?" he asked. I hesitated before, with a certain amount of embarrassment at the lofty suggestion, I requested Lightnings. He'd paused, looked me in the eye and grinned: "I don't see why not!"

I realised that my preference had been taken seriously when the posting notice arrived. I'd been instructed to report to RAF Valley where I would fly the Folland Gnat. The Gnat could reach supersonic airspeed in a shallow dive, a feat that I achieved just one week after my twenty-first birthday. After Valley I was sent to RAF Chivenor in Devon for the 'pre-Lightning' course on the Hawker Hunter. We were taught the techniques of how to aim and fire the

Hunter's four 30mm Aden cannon against a towed target, a difficult exercise; not many managed to gain high scores.

In September 1965 my ambition to fly Lightnings had materialised at last. I was posted to the Lightning Operational Conversion Unit at RAF Coltishall, a prospect that seemed slightly overwhelming if I'd thought about it too much. Sometimes, when not on duty, I would stand at the end of the Coltishall runway to take photographs of Lightnings as they performed circuits and overshoots. I could not avoid a warm feeling of achievement. For one thing, my course colleagues and I were among the first 'all-through' Lightning pilots; up to now only fighter pilots with experience on other aircraft types had been selected for Lightnings.

There'd been much to learn. Often, I read long into the night to study Pilots' Notes, bone up on technical manuals, absorb detailed documents on operating procedures. Sometimes fatigue would cause the light to swim under my eyes; words would seem to harden and slip off the page; whirlwinds of information would revolve irksomely around my head. The task, though, was imperative if I wanted to pass the course. Required standards had been high and obligatory; there'd been no short cuts. However, when prompt understanding had pierced the blur of fog, when the brain had grasped, as if a poignard had been thrust through the eye, a complex issue, the sense of satisfaction had been great.

Suddenly, I glanced again at my watch. Dave Hampton in his adjacent Lightning and the groundcrews all waited apprehensively for my signal. The moment has come, I thought, let's get going now. I raised one hand and gave a clear circling motion. At once, lethargy was thrust aside as everyone sprang into action. Both Lightnings were soon started and I called air traffic control for taxy and take-off clearance. Gnat training aircraft in the local airfield circuit were ordered to stay clear as priority was given to our esteemed Lightnings.

Before long, when both Lightnings were ready to roar off down the runway, Dave Hampton took off some seconds after me in the stiff cross-wind. After take-off, as I initiated a climb, simultaneously I turned port onto an easterly heading while Dave closed up to an echelon position for a period before he moved into a loose battle formation while we headed towards the Menai Straits. Soon, when we reached an altitude of 30,000 feet as instructed, I changed radio frequency to speak with the radar controller at RAF Aberporth, a military base north of Fishguard. This controller would give me instructions to intercept an unmanned target drone known as a Jindivik. Powered by the same Armstrong Siddeley Viper jet engine as that used in a Jet Provost aircraft, the Jindiviks were based at Llanbedr, a Royal Air Force station north of Aberystwyth on the coast of Cardigan Bay. Remotely controlled by personnel at Llanbedr, the Jindivik towed a magnesium flare attached to the end of a very long cable. When in missile-firing range, the Lightning pilot would call for the flare to be lit; the number two Lightning pilot would verify when this had happened. In theory, therefore, the Firestreak heat-seeking missile would strike the magnesium flare and not the expensive Jindivik which would be spared to fight another day. So much for the theory.

Firestreak missile launch at missile practice camp, RAF Valley, late 1960s. Note smoke trail of Jindivik in the background (Photo taken by Roger Beazley).

"Maintain your altitude and turn onto a heading of 150 degrees," said the controller in his lilting Welsh accent. On my right side, the Llyn Peninsular formed the northern boundary of Cardigan Bay; ahead, I could spot various lakes, including the distinctive four-mile long Bala lake, set within the Welsh mountains.

"The target is on your left, crossing left to right," said the controller. "Increase your airspeed slightly and standby for a right turn."

I nudged the Lightning's throttles forward: the engine revolutions edged up, the jet pipe temperatures reacted. I re-checked the altimeter...30,000 feet as required, no problems there. My airspeed had settled and the controller's calm voice commenced count-down: "The target is still on your left at a distance of ten miles," he said. I searched briefly but the small Jindivik was hard to make out. After a hasty glance at the other Lightning, I concentrated on accurate flying. Soon the controller went on: "Target now at eight miles, on your left side. Turn onto a heading of 170 degrees. This will be a 90-degree interception." I checked below as I turned and noted how the sea's slate-grey surface had been roughened by the wind. I searched again for the Jindivik but still failed to see the machine. Then, when the controller called: "Target now at a distance of five miles", I glimpsed at last the unconventional flying machine reminiscent of the V1 'doodlebugs' of WW2.

"Visual with the target," I told the controller.

"Copied," said the controller. Normally at this point I would have called 'Judy' to indicate that I'd assume control of the intercept geometry. Today, however, I would remain under close control – very close control – until I was ready to fire the missile.

"Commence a right turn now," said the controller after a pause. "Roll out on 260 degrees."

"Copied."

"The firing range is confirmed as clear," said the controller. "You're authorised to continue." Sometimes firings were held up at the last minute if shipping vessels had wandered into the range.

"The target is now three miles ahead of you," said the controller.

"Acknowledged." I carried out a further quick check around the cockpit to make sure that my 'switchery' was correctly set.

"Target at two miles." I made a nervous adjustment to my radar picture.

"Target at one-and-a-half miles."

"Light the flare!" I commanded.

After a moment or two, Dave Hampton cried: "Confirming that the flare has lit."

"You're clear to fire!" said the controller.

Now, with the target's range down to about one mile, I made a final check of my cockpit switches before I called excitedly: "*five...four...three...two... one...FIRING!*"

I was aware of a momentary pause, followed by a muffled bang. Then I saw the Firestreak accelerate ahead of my Lightning, a trail of smoke snaking behind the missile. The sight both startled and fascinated me; recollections of endless hours of interminable training seemed to career through my mind. It was as if justification of all that effort had been condensed into a fleeting interval of time. I felt elated, triumphant – but not for long. Abruptly, after about five seconds, the sense of jubilation was exchanged for thoughts like 'this can't be happening'. I knew that violence and destruction were about to succeed order and control: my recalcitrant Firestreak missile had bypassed the towed magnesium flare and locked itself onto the Jindivik's jet pipe. With a sense of dread, I witnessed an explosion followed by the Jindivik's sad, expensive remains fluttering down to the Irish Sea's surface below.

A stunned silence dominated the airwaves for what felt like an eternity. Meanwhile, I had to apply a high angle of bank to avoid dangerous clouds of debris. I knew that any kind of explanation to the controller would be superfluous: he would have deduced from his radar screen exactly what had happened. There was nothing to be done except turn towards Valley, initiate a descent and sneak back to base.

In the afternoon, for the second missile firing, Dave Hampton took the lead and I was his number two. As before, initial proceedings went well. The Aberporth controller set us up for the intercept and confirmed that no shipping vessels had wandered into the firing range. The parameters looked good, everything seemed wonderful. Until, that is, the point when Dave called for the magnesium flare to be lit. I stared intently ahead as he began a countdown to firing. The magnesium flare, however, failed to ignite; a second Jindivik was in dire peril. "Don't shoot!" I cried, an expression which, on reflection, seemed somewhat over-dramatic; perhaps I'd been watching too many cowboy films on TV. In any case, the call was wasted; Dave's countdown dominated the airwaves; no-one heard my warning. This time, the Jindivik's destruction was even more spectacular than before as Dave Hampton's missile, unlike mine, had been fitted with a full warhead.

That evening in the officers' mess, when I went through recent matters in my mind, I could not avoid tiresome twinges of guilt. It had been quite a day – a day of expensive errors in hapless succession. While the misfortunes had hardly been my fault, the weight of conscience seemed to bear down on me like a storm cloud. But then, I thought suddenly, perhaps I should concentrate on the bright side of things. I should maintain a positive attitude, just as I'd learned at Cranwell. After all, I was one of life's optimists; a confident type; a glass-half-full merchant. I would live to shoot another day.

CHAPTER 16

KEPT WAITING

23 Squadron Mk 6, which Squadron Leader Ed Durham flew to Canada in 1968, prior to the squadron's deployment at RAF Masirah.

CLIFF ROBINSON'S LATE ARRIVAL

It seemed mighty odd. Admittedly, we were sleep deprived and probably devoid of inspiration, even so to start just one out of twelve Rolls-Royce engines appeared a somewhat humble accomplishment. I glanced across at my fellow Lightning pilot. We sat in our Lightning cockpits at Esenboğa airport, some twenty miles north of Ankara in central Turkey, but he seemed as uncertain as the rest of us what to do next. All six of our 23(F) Squadron Lightnings were due for an early departure from Esenboğa from where we planned to fly to Hamadan airport in north-western Iran. Yesterday, supported by in-flight refuelling Victor tankers, we had flown directly to Esenboğa airport from our base at RAF Leuchars in Scotland. Following our overnight stop in Turkey we'd been programmed to fly a series of short legs without the Victors' support. Our aim, eventually, was to reach RAF Masirah on the northern tip of the small island of Masirah off the coast of Oman. Once there, we would take part in an air defence exercise in co-operation with the Royal Air Force of Oman. At present, however, it appeared that we were about to go nowhere fast. This was not good news; our schedule was tight.

The ground crewman allocated to my aircraft climbed the Lightning's cockpit access ladder with a message. "It's not looking good, sir," he said. "The starter systems are buggered."

"All of them?"

"Yes. All of them."

"Tremendous!" I said. I raised my eyes to the skies but he merely shrugged his shoulders.

Now, as all six pilots climbed out of their cockpits for the problem to be investigated by engineering experts, we knew that we were in for a long delay. There was little choice, therefore, but to be driven back to our hotel in central Ankara while we awaited developments. In some ways, this was not such a bad thing. We'd have a reasonable excuse to recover from the previous night's excesses. Most unusually for Fighter Command aircrews, we had been booked in to a luxurious four-star hotel in downtown Ankara; normally, such treatment was the preserve of Transport Command crews and their illustrious airline counterparts.

Last night, I had been intrigued by the sight of two dancing bears on the street outside our hotel. Attended by two old men, their faces sallow above thin, silvery hair which was long and wispy at the back, the bears appeared to accept without protest endless prods and pokes with sticks. It occurred to me that the enormous bears could have overpowered their keepers with ease, but I heard later that the bears' teeth and claws had been removed to render the creatures virtually defenceless.

After a civilised dinner in the hotel, four of our group of Lightning pilots had decided to walk around Ankara in search of a nightclub. It was a fine spring evening in late March 1969; we were young, impetuous, indestructible.

The main streets of Ankara had been well lit and occupied by generally respectable-looking types staring at window displays of shoe shops, clothing stores, tattoo parlours, exotic carpet shops. Some of the back streets, though, had been littered with discarded drink cans and over-run by gangs of brown cats that walked across the refuse. We hurried past men and women, moist and fat, who eyed us with suspicion as they sat on doorsteps, but we had accepted that the rotten, pervasive smell and the less-than-salubrious atmosphere were part of life's rich pattern. Eventually we chanced across a fairly lavish-looking nightclub and decided to make our way inside. Shown to a table by a uniformed attendant, we felt awkward at first and there was little conversation. None of us could speak a word of Turkish but we managed, nonetheless, to order four beers which were served quite promptly. I watched the pilot opposite me as he leant forward to draw lines with his finger across the dew of his cold beer glass.

I gazed around the room to observe the nightclub's other guests. At an adjacent table I noticed a young woman's coy smile as she looked, with her most calculatedly fetching sideways glance, at her not-so-youthful admirer. Another table was occupied by a group of young women, one of whom started to pull up a stocking when she suddenly caught sight of me watching her. She stopped what she was doing and sat there with her leg out straight, the stocking half-pulled up. Another girl was applying lipstick to her lips. Her friend used a small mirror to check her hair. All of the girls were in shiny Turkish evening dress, glossy gold or blue baubled or lustrous green.

"The show should start soon," said one of our party.

"When?"

"Dunno, but it must be soon."

We ordered more beer and stared yearningly at the small stage on one side of the room. Despite strident attempts by the nightclub's pre-recorded music of bowed fiddle, plucked zither and kudüm drum to lure the mind towards suggestive Ottoman harem belly dancers with sensual fingers and pelvic thrusts, the stage remained determinedly vacant. The nightclub's atmosphere stayed rather subdued; the room had become hot, stuffy, airless. We wondered whether to move on to another establishment, but the beer was acceptable and the heat had nibbled at the mind's indecision. Towards midnight, one of our pilots nodded off, then woke with a start. It was a curious moment; the half-waking chaos of an involuntary late-night nap fogged the brain and he seemed alarmed by his abrupt transportation into a room where the air was filled with the stickiness of aroused desire. Fantasy, unreason and lust grew best in the heat.

There appeared to be some, if not all, of these in abundance at the table next to ours. Although we'd not understood any words drifting across, a creative imagination provided a compelling substitute. It was as if, I reckoned, the young woman's companion had seen the light of hopefulness in her eyes and been impressed. He'd waved his arms about when ready to say something, then stopped in mid-flourish to make a sceptical noise in the back of his throat. His face had seemed to brighten; I noticed a charming, chipped-tooth smile and he tapped the side of his rather large Turkish nose. "Occasionally my memory fails me," I imagined the conversation, "but not for long." I'm sure that I saw a pronounced wink of one eye

"Oh good," she might have replied; her eyes had appeared to twinkle as she went to kiss him coquettishly on that nose.

All of this, of course, had been a mere distraction – an impromptu sideshow as we waited for the main show to commence. By 2am, after the use of elaborate hand signals, we had managed, finally, to elicit the information from a waiter that the show would commence at 3am. We held a hasty conference to decide what to do next. An early start was planned – a 6am pick-up from the hotel. It had been a long day and maybe we should return to the hotel for some sleep. The thought-processes, though, had wandered quite quickly from this sensible strategy: to hell with it, we agreed eventually; we're young, impetuous and all of those other good things. Anyway, we'd waited long enough for this bloody show to commence and if it meant another hour's delay...well, so what?

That next hour seemed to pass slowly. By 2.30am my head started to throb. Someone shouted across the room and the sound startled me. By 2.45am I wanted to grasp my hands on top of my head which had begun to spin around and around until I felt like falling over in a dizzy heap on the ground. By 3.05am we'd almost reached the point of giving up when, suddenly, a belly dancer burst through parted curtains at the back of the stage. The entire room came alive in an instant. To enthusiastic applause she side-stepped nimbly across the stage as she twirled her skirts. With her arms above her head she arched her body backwards. Then, her fingers crooked, she allowed her black tresses to tumble down the top part of her back. At length, the music slowed to a deliberate, rhythmic beat as she placed her hands on her hips and gyrated her body expertly in time with the harmony. The women in the audience, I noticed, looked a little uncomfortable but the men wore expressions of glazed satisfaction. Apart, that is, from one: a Lightning pilot in our group had fallen asleep just as the show was about to begin. Other dancers appeared on the stage, all of whom managed to exhaust themselves in one way or another. Later, we discovered that the dancers had come from Doncaster (yes, Doncaster). The activities of the devilish Dervish dancers from Doncaster (and why not?) had sent the local male clientele into frenzies of appreciation even though we'd had our doubts. At around 4am, by which time we'd made it back to our hotel, my head still throbbed and I felt a bit sick.

The subsequent engine starting saga at Esenboğa airport, although for some a lucky break for all the wrong reasons, was causing eruptions in the engineering world. Heads were scratched, manuals scoured, conferences held; everyone claimed to be foxed. Then some bright spark realised that the altitude of Esenboğa airport, at 3,200 feet, was approximately 3,200 feet higher than the height recommended in the Lightning's Release to Service document. This document, give or take a bit of self-interest here, a perceptual distortion there, an inky ambiguity in this place or that, still warned that the aircraft should be operated only out of airfields at sea level.

Having discovered the cause of the problem, time was needed to devise a solution. Another two nights at the Ankara hotel plus a further visit to our favourite nightclub meant that we pilots became progressively more sleep deprived. Meanwhile, one of our detachment engineers, a brave and ingenious individual, had discovered that by blowing with his mouth into the top of the 'Avpin' starter tank he'd managed to pressurise the air space in the top part of the tank. This did the trick; the engines started; it was a 'eureka' moment. However, as Avpin (isopropyl nitrate colourless monopropellant) was a highly toxic, highly flammable, highly explosive, highly awful liquid, blowing into the tank was not considered a good idea. A Heath Robinson device, therefore, was rigged up using oxygen cylinders, pressure regulators and a random selection of seals found in various toolboxes. The device proved successful, the engines started and the next day, at last, we took off for Hamadan airport in Iran.

Our route, north of Syria to Tabriz before a right turn for Hamadan, took us over disparate, largely barren, territories. As we approached Hamadan, we picked up two airborne contacts which turned out to be Iranian air force Northrop F5 Freedom Fighter aircraft. With our Lightning over-wing fuel tanks, our maximum airspeed was meant to be limited but under the circumstances we decided to ignore the limit. Some thirty miles north of Hamadan airport a plaintive voice came over the airwaves:

"Lightnings aircraft flying to Hamadan...theese ees Iranian air force F5 commander."

"You're loud and clear," I said.

"Pleese slow down. We are here to welcome you but we cannot catch up!"

The welcome at Hamadan was impressive but we had no time to linger; our next stop, RAF Sharjah in the Trucial States (nowadays the United Arab Emirates) on the southern expanses of the Persian Gulf, had to be reached by late afternoon.

We touched down at Sharjah before sundown as planned but were surprised, after landing, to find few signs of the resident Hawker Hunter squadron members. We must have been the first Lightnings to have passed through the base which maybe explained why, eventually, the shy Hunter lads were lured out of hiding. After a somewhat sniffy inspection of our shiny steeds, the atmosphere gradually eased as both Hunter and Lightning boys began to realise that they had, after all, a fair bit in common.

In the officers' mess that evening I had an enlightening conversation with a couple of Hunter pilots who explained that, in view of their single-engined aircraft, they received regular and serious briefings on desert survival techniques. In their extreme environment, they said, the basic principles of survival – protection, location, water, food – became particularly significant. A Hunter pilot forced to bale out over the desert would face a precarious plight not just because of his lone situation but also because search and rescue facilities were notoriously limited.

There were other hazards too. Great areas of barrenness would be occupied by scorpions, lethal snakes, the occasional lizard, fast-moving spiders and scavenging dung beetles. By dusk, the wildlife would be attracted to any campsite fire which, if possible, should be lit when the air became sharp with the nip of nightfall. Night-time temperatures would plummet – a stark and perilous contrast to the stifling heat of day. If, before sundown, tribesmen and their camels appeared on the horizon, the pilots were advised, on making contact, to offer so-called 'goolie chits' which promised rewards for the pilot's safe return. Not all of the tribesmen were friendly but it was hoped that some of them, hardy desert folk with lean, hawk-like faces turned chestnut brown by the sun, would be sympathetic.

Chance meetings with tribesmen were rare, though, and a pilot still on his own by nightfall would have to adopt special strategies. If his campfire began to die down, the pilot should try to seek refuge, perhaps in the temporary shelter he had built in the day. Sleep, though, could be elusive. He might listen to the sough of wind through nearby sand dunes, stare up at the celestial panoply if the night sky was clear, watch shooting stars that arced above – sometimes fast and bright and extinguished in less than a second, sometimes slow and deliberate as if choosing with care a course across the galaxy. In this Lawrence of Arabia territory, the pilot might marvel at an existence that seemed to come straight from the 42nd psalm.

If my conversation had proved educational, it was the next day, as the Lightnings took off from Sharjah, that I was conscious of the Hunter boys' emphasis on potential local hazards. I felt awed by the landscape below. Devoid of towns and villages, the vast sandy stretches and reddish-coloured mountains and valleys seemed aptly named the 'empty quarter'.

When, at last, the Lightnings landed at Masirah, we knew that many lessons had been learned. Perhaps we were embarrassed about the course of events over the last few days: we spoke little between ourselves of the deployment experiences, and when we got home we did not talk about it all (in some cases, not for another forty years). We tried to busy ourselves at Masirah as the Lightnings' over-wing fuel tanks were removed, sector familiarisation flights were planned, and we thought about comprehensive exercise briefings. However, it was to no avail. One small but insuperable detail remained: we'd arrived too late to participate. The air defence exercise was over. It was time to go home.

CHAPTER 17

DIFFICULT DECISIONS

92 Squadron pilots L-R: Colin Armstrong, John Richardson, Dougie Aylward, Paddy Roberts, Rick McKnight, Ed Stein, John Holdway, Tim Cohu, Joseph Gilbert, Jim Carbourne, Chris Bruce, Sam Lucas, Geoff Denny, David Cousins, Jerry Bowler, John Rooum.

SIR JOSEPH (JOE) GILBERT IS REQUIRED TO SIGN

The young officer sidled up to my desk with a stealthy, soft-treaded gait. He knew that I would not be happy. That was apparent from the anxious movement of his small dark eyes which revealed that he knew that I knew.

"Yes?" I said.

"Your signature is required, sir," he said. "Right there, please, at the bottom of the file." He pointed.

"Okay, leave it with me."

The young officer seemed to make no sound at all as he crept out of my office. I may have stared long and hard at the file, tried to put off reading the contents, I don't really remember. I do recall, though, that when, eventually, I saw with my own eyes what I had suspected all along – that Lightning Mk 2 and Mk 2A aircraft were to be written off from service with the Royal Air Force and offered for use as gate guardians and other such ill-judged purposes – I experienced a deep and ominous sense of disquiet. As the 'Ministry Man', the air-vice marshal in the post of assistant chief of air staff (policy), it was my job to sign the final dire document that would, in effect, consign fine, formidable fighter aircraft to the scrap heap. This, in my opinion, was a wanton waste of resources, an imprudent measure, a misguided squandering of assets. To add insult to injury, I had flown some of these Lightnings personally when I was the commanding officer of 92 (East India) Squadron.

When I thought back, I knew that I'd been lucky to have been offered that 92 Squadron post. With a background flying Gloster Meteor, de Havilland Vampire and Gloster Javelin aircraft in the 1950s, I was a reasonably experienced fighter pilot, but seniority had seemed to conspire against my repeated requests for a posting to Lightnings. I was conscious of a particular incident which had sparked my desire to fly the aircraft. As a Javelin pilot in the early 1960s, I'd taken part in an air defence exercise. Known as the 'Dragmaster', the delta-wing Javelin with its massive T-tail was incapable of intercepting targets above embarrassingly restrictive heights and airspeeds. This made the prospect of dealing with earnest enemy efforts seem somewhat unrealistic, to put it mildly. One day during the exercise I watched with absolute amazement when a Lightning flew alongside my Javelin, then swiftly and with the greatest of ease switched from one target to the next before zooming off to return to base.

After this I applied to join the Lightning force, although my chances of success had appeared increasingly remote. I'd almost given up the idea until a prompt change of air force policy gave me a sudden and unexpected opportunity: in future, it was decreed, commanding officers of Lightning squadrons would be in the rank of wing commander instead of squadron leader. Although a generally unpopular move, this meant that from my point of view as a newly-promoted wing commander after staff college, I was presented with a very lucky break indeed. My posting as commanding officer of 92 Squadron which, among other matters, would involve the squadron's move from Leconfield in the East Riding of Yorkshire to Geilenkirchen in Germany (close to the German-Dutch border), would be at once prestigious and challenging.

As, normally, a pilot would not have taken command of a Lightning squadron without previous experience on the aircraft, I began my new job on 92 Squadron with a fair degree of trepidation. After the Lightning conversion course at RAF Coltishall, I needed to become 'combat ready' as swiftly as possible. When still fairly new on the squadron, I'd flown a pairs sortie led by an ex-Red Arrows display pilot – a flight that I would not forget. As he'd led me back to base, the ex-Red Arrows appeared to get a little carried away, so much so that I wondered if he'd forgotten that he was leading a 'new boy' and that, instead, he was back in the display team. As we cavorted about the sky I needed all of my powers of concentration to stay in position. Nonetheless, stay in position I did. At the end of the sortie, despite a sense of serious exhaustion, I felt as if I'd somehow passed an informal yet significant test the results of which, although unspoken, proved to the other squadron pilots that I could, indeed, fly the Lightning.

I had been with 92 Squadron for just three months when the squadron move to Geilenkirchen took place. We soon settled in to our new home, a well-planned airbase with a good long runway, fine local facilities and first-rate squadron accommodation. The day after our arrival, when the commander-in-chief of RAF Germany visited the squadron, he admired our Lightnings' colour scheme – the royal blue spine and tail with the squadron crest of a cobra (to represent that 92 Squadron was an East India gift squadron) and a maple leaf (to signify the squadron's association with Canada in WW1) painted boldly on the tail. Unaware of plans made by his staff, the commander-in-chief agreed that we should keep our colour scheme without alteration – an authorisation taken literally for the rest of the squadron's time in Germany.

When declared 'combat ready' I would take my turn to hold readiness in the so-called Battle Flight set-up at Royal Air Force Gütersloh with two Lightnings fully armed and prepared to be airborne at short notice. One night, not long after I had commenced Battle Flight duty, the 'squawk box' in one corner of the pilots' small crew room crackled abruptly into life. "*Gütersloh, alert one Lightning*," the controller demanded.

At once, the other pilot acknowledged the order and activated the scramble alarm while, as the allocated 'Q1' (the first to be scrambled), I dashed to my Lightning. Careful cockpit preparation assisted speedy progress as I leapt up the cockpit access ladder steps two at a time, hastily plugged in my PEC (personal equipment connector), placed my bone dome on my head and checked-in with the controller. "Vector 035 degrees, climb to 36,000 feet...*scramble*," the controller cried breathlessly. Clearly, the situation was urgent – a border infringement between East and West Germany, perhaps, or a pilot with some airborne emergency who needed assistance.

A member of groundcrew, having helped me to strap in, removed and stowed my ejection seat safety pins, slid rapidly down the cockpit access ladder, removed the ladder and stood to one side while I started my Rolls-Royce Avon engines. The procedure, slick and well rehearsed, ensured that I was soon ready to taxy towards the runway at which point air traffic control cleared me for immediate take-off. Still fairly new to Lightnings, I felt a sense of thrill from the punch in the back caused when the reheats were engaged during the take-off run. My peripheral vision picked up a blur of lights to each side as the Lightning accelerated down the pitch-black runway.

Once airborne, I checked in with the GCI (ground control intercept) controller who ordered me to continue to climb as I held a north-easterly course. I made frequent checks around the cockpit to confirm that my radar and other systems remained serviceable, and I adjusted my cockpit lighting to reduce the brightness: a night visident (visual identification) involved special hazards and I needed to plan well ahead, including the acclimatisation of my eyes to darker conditions. As the Lightning headed progressively further from base I began to feel apprehensive about my fuel state. When I mentioned this to the controller he merely said: "Turn left now onto a heading of 020 degrees." No doubt his priority had been focussed on a successful interception even if my low fuel state had meant an eventual diversion away from base.

"Copied," I said, shortly followed by: "rolling out on a heading of 020 degrees."

With the Lightning now adjacent to the 'buffer zone', the controller waited a few moments before instructing me to turn a further ten degrees to the left. He was under strict orders to ensure that I didn't fly too close to the East/West German border. "Your target is currently fifteen miles ahead on your right side," the controller went on, "descend to 32,000 feet."

I peered anxiously at my small radar screen. The screen, though, was flooded with a variety of complex green radar 'paints' and the picture was hard to interpret.

"You are closing on the target," the controller said, "he's presently ten miles ahead on your right side and slightly above."

With my left hand I used the Lightning's hand controller to make continuous minor radar adjustments but the target, still hidden within radar clutter, remained hard to pick out. However, when the controller said: "Your target's now just over five miles ahead," I became convinced that a particular 'blip' seemed to coincide with the controller's ongoing patter. Before long, when the controller's instructions had verified this beyond doubt, I was able to call 'Judy'– no further instructions needed from ground control. I concentrated then on manoeuvring the Lightning for optimum visual identification of the target. On most nights, a lighter section of sky or a particular cluster of bright stars or perhaps the moon could be used to advantage. I had to fly with finesse;

harsh control movements could have led to difficulty. At length, though, as I approached stealthily from astern and as I employed nature's luminous backcloth to highlight the target's silhouette, I was able to identify a Soviet Tupolev Tu-104 (NATO code-named 'Camel'), a civil airliner version of the twin-engined, swept wing Tupolev Tu-16 bomber (NATO code-named 'Badger').

When I reported this to the controller, he ordered me to break off the interception. Later, I learnt that the Camel had strayed by mistake across the East/West German border. At the time, though, as the interception had taken me too far north for a return to base, I elected to divert to Hanover airport for a refuel. I found the set-up at Hanover to be efficient and helpful, and I noted, too, that my fully-armed Lightning with its striking royal blue paintwork caused quite a stir.

Not long after this Battle Flight interception, 92 Squadron became involved in a NATO air defence exercise. I recall a particular sortie to intercept a high-speed, high-altitude target which turned out to be a Luftwaffe F104 Starfighter (an aircraft, incidentally, which had been introduced into service at about the same time as the Lightning but which had remained in operational service with some air forces for over fifteen years longer than the Lightning in the Royal Air Force – some justification, perhaps, for my strongly-held views against writing off our Lightnings prematurely). The high fuel consumption involved with the interception of this F104 meant that my flight time for the sortie amounted to a grand total of twenty-four minutes.

Another short flight loomed when, towards the end of the air defence exercise, I was scrambled to intercept a target at '40,000 feet plus'. I hastened through the start-up and take-off procedures after which, having been cleared by air traffic control, I commenced a climb towards the target. Just as I passed through an altitude of around 14,000 feet my attention was drawn to the cockpit warning panel as 'clang – clang – clang' reverberated within my headset earpieces. A glance at the warning panel revealed that I had suffered a 'FIRE 1' – fire in number one engine. At once, I throttled back both engines to reduce speed and carry out emergency drills, including operation of the number one engine fire extinguisher. Fortunately this worked and after a short delay the fire warning light dimmed before going out.

I'd put out an emergency 'PAN' call to which the controller had responded that the airfield approach was clear and that fire services had been alerted. My subsequent approach and landing proceeded without further problems except that, after landing and shut down when I was assisted with cockpit evacuation by fire crews, I felt the need to sit down on a nearby grassy stretch. At that point, the Geilenkirchen fire officer came up to me to offer a lift back to the squadron buildings. "Thanks, Rick," I said gratefully, but when I attempted to stand up my legs just gave way. At once, the fire officer, instead of making a fuss, calmly helped me to sit down again before he, too, sat down next to me on the grass. The two of us remained there for a good fifteen or twenty minutes quietly chatting away while the perspicacious and kindly fire officer gave my system a chance to recover from the effects of delayed shock.

A shock to my system came in another form when it was time for me to leave 92 Squadron. I felt lost. As the commanding officer of a Lightning squadron, my life had seemed about as good as it could get and I'd been in a quandary about what I should do next. Rescue came from a somewhat unexpected quarter when Air Vice-Marshal Neil Cameron (later Marshal of the Royal Air Force Baron Cameron of Balhousie, chief of defence staff) asked me to join his newly-formed defence policy staff.

After three-and-a half years in this job, which had given me a new interest when I'd developed expertise in nuclear defence policy, I was posted to Royal Air Force Coltishall, Norfolk as station commander. I managed to achieve around ten to fifteen flying hours a month at Coltishall where I enjoyed flying the so-called 'Loony Lightning'. This form of modified Lightning had been stripped of its radar and fitted instead with a Luneburg lens, a spherically symmetrical device with a metallic surface. The Loony Lightnings with their improved radar reflective properties assisted students to learn the art of intercept geometry.

After Coltishall I'd been saddened to lose my last links with the Lightning. In a future job as the air officer commanding of 38 Group I was able to fly a number of different aircraft types, but not the Lightning. This remained a matter of regret because for me, without doubt, the Lightning had always been (and always would be) by far my favourite aircraft to fly. That may have been on my mind when the young officer sidled up to my desk to ask for a signature. A number of factors now fuelled my intransigence and mood of intense exasperation as I persisted with my refusal to sign away valuable Mk 2 and Mk 2A Lightnings.

An intriguing series of visitors began to visit me in my office. A squadron leader, followed by a wing commander then a group captain all traipsed into the office one by one, all with long faces and all determined to persuade me to sign. Eventually an air commodore entered. "Boss," he said, "you really must sign this file. We don't have any choice." I begged to differ.

It was later in the day when the matter reached the ministry's higher echelons. A squawk box on my desk sprang abruptly into life; a small light indicated that the vice-chief of the air staff himself now demanded my immediate attention.

I flicked a switch. "Sir?" I said.

"You're playing silly buggers," he said. There was more than a touch of irritation in his voice. I imagined a face drawn and pale, the skin almost grey, the eyes focussed somewhere out in front. Firmly and politely I tried to put my case – a mix of operational, sentimental and practical reasons.

"The decision's already been made," growled the vice-chief of the air staff. "Your signature is a mere formality." In the ensuing moments of silence I could picture squabbling seagulls wheel and scream before they disappeared in the mist. A few shadowy figures appeared to rise out of the mists then fade away again like so many lost souls.

"I'm sorry, sir," I said eventually. Into the awkward recesses of my mind there penetrated a slow, delayed echo of his voice as the vice-chief of the air staff concluded our conversation.

"You're still refusing to sign?" he said.

"Yes."

At this, I was aware of a click when, without further ado, the vice-chief switched off his squawk box. It seemed that, regretfully, I'd forgone any possible aspirations to become the ministry's next 'employee of the month'. There was something deadening and robotic about the whole affair. I'd probably have to carry the scars of my decision, but at least I could feel that a certain sense of honour had been retained.

Some time later I learned that the vice-chief of the air staff had himself signed the required paperwork. My career went on to include that of deputy air officer commanding Royal Air Force Strike Command, then deputy commander-in-chief of Allied Forces Northern Europe before I retired from the service in 1989. Since that time, I have served as president internationally of the Royal Air Force Association, prime minister's trustee on the board of the Imperial War Museum and – the best thing since retirement – vice-chairman of the Commonwealth War Graves Commission.

Nowadays, as I am in what might be termed 'deep retirement', I act as a part-time guide at the thirteenth-century Salisbury Cathedral in Wiltshire. On duty there every Tuesday morning, I'd be delighted to meet anyone who wishes to approach me to 'talk Lightnings'. I have the greatest respect for the Lightning boys. I feel proud to have been one of them. I'm glad that I refused to sign that odious piece of paper.

CHAPTER 18

TOPSY-TURVY

Line up of 56(F) Squadron Lightnings.

ROGER COLEBROOK'S FLIGHT INSTRUMENT PROBLEMS

The process started slowly, insidiously, which was perhaps why I didn't realise at first. It was dark and overcast beyond the southern coast of Cyprus on that April night in 1968. Above my Lightning's position over the sea, layers of cloud meant that I lacked the benefit of background moon and stars to aid orientation. In spite of this, I soon settled into my search pattern, pressed my head against the radar display's rubber hood and adjusted my pistol-grip hand controller with its complex collection of a dozen or so buttons, thumbwheels and switches used to manage the Lightning's radar system. When settled at a height of 1,500 feet in level flight, I flicked, instinctively, the 'attitude hold' mode of the Lightning's rudimentary autopilot. Use of this facility was restricted to heights above 5,000 feet but my high workload caused a momentary lapse of memory and on a night like this I needed all the help I could get.

As I stared at the small radar screen, I began to make out what I thought might be a target to the right. I made another minor adjustment on the hand controller and continued to gaze at the screen.

Gradually, however, the radar picture began to change. The screen's sea returns now slowly, subtly assumed an unusual slant; the picture started to look distinctly odd. My initial reaction was that I'd been subjected to radar 'jamming' – our 56(F) Squadron pilots had been briefed to anticipate electronic counter measures during the exercise. I concentrated intently as I strived to interpret the radar. I might even have become transfixed. As my balance organs began to doubt the visual information fed to my eyes and brain, I sensed an alarming disconnect between mind and reality. My uneasiness grew; my pulse quickened. It was as if a fine tremolo of trumpets and violins had started suddenly to sound like cats, a yard full of them, all yowling *danger...danger...danger*. In an instant, I snapped my head away from the radar hood. My heart raced; I hesitated momentarily as I tried to work out what was happening but a glance at the altimeter revealed that I was just seconds from disaster. My corrective action was immediate and violent.

It was about a year before this incident that rumours of 56(F) Squadron's possible permanent deployment to Cyprus in the spring of 1967 eventually translated into reality. I'd joined the squadron in February of that year and soon became caught up in the widespread air of excitement as postings officers from HQ visited us, futures were discussed, and information was circulated about our new base at Akrotiri on the southern tip of the island. In my own case, however, I had reservations. When summonsed to my flight commander's office to discuss the issue, I entered politely and offered my best military salute along with a pleasant, goofy smile. "Looks as if we're all lined up for plum postings, young Roger," my flight commander said cheerily.

I gazed at my flight commander. He was well aware that Yusha, my five-stone family dog, relied on me for a home. When I was flying, Yusha usually slept under a table until I returned. Normally well-behaved, the dog, though, could be protective if provoked. One time, for instance, an instructor at my advanced flying course at RAF Valley, a rather unpleasant individual, had tried to berate me for something or other when I noticed that his high-pitched voice had changed abruptly to a strangled yelp, his face had contorted and he'd dropped to his knees. It was then when I saw that Yusha had grabbed the instructor by the seat of his trousers and dragged him to the floor.

An ominous pause ensued. My flight commander's cheery expression changed to an irritated scowl. "Well that's just too bad, Roger," he said eventually in reaction to my misgivings. “Like it or not, you’re bloody well going and that’s that.” At this, I was summarily dismissed from the flight commander’s presence.

After this, I tried to ‘think positive’. Apart from the benefits of the Cypriot climate, I reckoned that the tenuous Middle East situation would be bound to ensure a stimulating operational environment for our squadron. We couldn’t have known, of course, that our move in April 1967 was just two months before the outbreak of the Six-Day Arab-Israeli war.

The squadron’s marathon move had gone well for most, although we heard later of a slight *contretemps* between the squadron’s commanding officer and our new qualified flying instructor who together flew the two-seat Lightning T5 to Cyprus. The CO had acquired a novel device, a kneepad arrangement, filled with customised charts and checklists. Designed especially for the trip, the CO was mighty proud of his new contraption. Regretfully, however, the device was a bit too bulky for the cramped confines of a Lightning cockpit. As a result, the good wing commander, unable to strap his pride-and-joy to his knee, had been obliged to place the thing between the Lightning T5’s two ejection seats. This had worked reasonably well until an hour or two into the trip when the flying instructor had decided to adjust the height of his seat. A graunching noise, heard even above the background racket within the Lightning’s cockpit, had been accompanied by the CO’s expression of horror when, in an instant, his new-fangled but now-mangled gadget was rendered useless – as useless, indeed, as some had declared all along.

As the squadron settled in to its new situation, we soon began to appreciate just how stark was the disparity between our current Middle East environment and that of our former base at Wattisham in leafy, sleepy Suffolk. As the Cypriot noonday heat could become quite overpowering, often we would aim to start a day’s work early in the morning and finish by lunchtime. Sometimes, first thing, I would look out from the squadron set-up to admire our new surroundings. Terrain around Akrotiri itself was flat but to the north the peak of Mount Olympus at 6,400 feet would offer, on a clear day, a spectacular navigational aid for us newly-arrived pilots. From Fassouri plantation, just north of Akrotiri, the sweet smell of orange blossom would drift across the airfield to provide an incongruous blend with the airfield’s whiff of high octane aviation fuel.

I liked to look up into the sky and listen to the faint, far-off pounding of the sea upon the beaches. Intermixed with the shrill hubbub of spring birdsong, the assortment of sounds produced a strange, intoxicating atmosphere. In contrast to nature’s best, the black surface of the runway stood out as a dark scar set between sandy-coloured grasses. The east-west runway, which pointed towards tourist beaches and the waters of the Mediterranean Sea, would shimmer in the noon sun; heat haze would hang languidly over the airfield. Sometimes, on the hottest of days, we could feel the burning air touch the inside of our lungs. The sun would bear down on shoulders and backs; our shirts would offer scant protection as perspiration trickled down from necks, over chests to be collected by waist-belts.

We had been in Cyprus a mere matter of weeks when it became obvious that Arab-Israeli posturing was about to develop into full-scale war. Egypt had started to amass troops and tanks in the Sinai; Syria and Jordan had sent troops in large numbers to reinforce border areas; the population of Israel had begun to dig fortifications and to make preparations to evacuate children to Europe. Later, we would learn that Israeli air force pilots had been extensively schooled about their planned targets in Egypt. Furthermore, the pilots had been made to memorise every detail of these targets as well as rehearsing, in total secrecy, attack profiles on dummy runways.

On the morning of 5th June 1967, coincident with civil defence sirens sounding across Israel, all but twelve of the Israeli air force's nearly two hundred operational jet aircraft launched a mass attack against Egyptian airfields. The Israeli pilots flew low across the sea to avoid radar detection, the Egyptian air defence infrastructure was poor and the Egyptian aircraft, partly due to the efforts of a double agent, had been left in the open making them vulnerable to air attack. The outcome was dramatic; it was estimated later that over 300 Egyptian aircraft had been destroyed and around 100 Egyptian pilots killed; in a bold stroke, Israel had gained air superiority for the period of the war.

From my own point of view, as I'd been with the squadron for such a short period and my status was non-operational, I was not allowed to fly other than on training sorties. Nonetheless, I'd been on duty for other squadron tasks that morning and witnessed the scene when one of our operational pilots was scrambled to intercept an aircraft of unknown origin to the south of Cyprus heading towards Israel. The intruder had been reported to be at low level and a judicious approach was required. Our man had closed up stealthily from astern to identify a Nord Noratlas N-2501D with Israeli markings; Israel had purchased 16 of these aircraft before the war. It turned out that the Noratlas was being used to provide survival support for Israeli air force crews who may have had to ditch in the sea after their pre-emptive raids against Egypt. As the role of the Lightnings in Cyprus was restricted to protection of the sovereign base areas on the island, our man had taken no action other than to report back details of his interception. Over the next days our squadron pilots carried out a large number of unusual interceptions and we were warned about the possibility of defectors from Israel's neighbours wishing to seek the safe haven of Akrotiri.

Later in the year, some months after the conclusion of the Arab-Israeli conflict, I became involved in unusual interceptions of a different kind. By that stage I had been declared operational and, along with other squadron pilots, I'd been scrambled on a number of occasions to intercept aircraft of the Turkish air force which, in support of Turkey's contested claims over parts of Cyprus, had begun to send flights over the island's northern areas. Our Lightnings would intercept such flights although our rules of engagement dictated that we could engage the intruders only if they fired at us first, or if they attacked ground targets. As the Turkish pilots were notoriously bad at lookout, we would enjoy opportunities to stalk them and to see how much time elapsed before our presence was discovered. Several of our pilots would report how they'd been able to remain in a close line astern position undetected for a considerable period. Once discovered, however, some amazing tail-chases would ensue against, in the main, RF 84-F Thunderflash photo-reconnaissance aircraft and Lockheed F104 Starfighters.

One time, I was chasing a low-level RF 84-F flying due north from Kyrenia when I suddenly spotted something abnormal-looking on the horizon. At first I thought it was the distant coastline but as I flew closer I could discern a large fleet of naval ships. My God, I thought, that's the Turkish invasion fleet on its way to Cyprus. The RF 84-F, presumably in radio contact with the fleet, had overflown with impunity but I decided that, with my own prospects likely to be distinctly less promising, I should veer away. I then held a safe distance and noted as many details as I could before dashing back to base to make an urgent report. The intelligence team told me that they'd been monitoring the fleet for several days but, in the end, it was not until 1974 that the Turks finally decided to invade Cyprus.

Although tit-for-tat Arab/Israeli raids following the Six-Day War had continued into 1968, most of these flights were too distant for our Lightnings to become involved. Our training schedule, therefore, continued as training schedules are inclined to do, including the inevitable round of pre-planned exercises. One of these, the peculiarly-named Exercise Crayon, was an air defence exercise designed to last for several days in April 1968. The exercise planners had concentrated on a hypothetical threat from low-flying targets.

When, at around midnight, I was scrambled to take up my allocated slot in the fighter combat air patrol pattern, I was well aware of the need to be mindful of adjacent fighters. The squadron had devised a system which offered optimum coverage of as large an area as possible by using the combined radars of a number of Lightnings. Each individual Lightning pilot, therefore, had to maintain accurate orientation within the overall patrol pattern. This requirement, however, added further to the already-complicated parameters under which we operated.

As I now persisted with necessary time, distance, wind and other calculations to hold my position, I ruminated on the woeful limitations of the Lightning's radar at low level. At high altitude, I would hope to detect a medium-sized target at a range of 25 or more miles, but at low level over a calm sea the detection distance was reduced to about ten miles, sometimes as little as two miles if the sea state was rough. Over land, ground returns rendered the radar virtually useless at low level.

To assist during an interception, my radar screen displayed a gyro-operated artificial horizon. It was this system, or perhaps I should say the failure of this system, which was about to lead me into trouble. In the course of ongoing positional calculations I thought that I spotted a faint 'blip' on the right-hand edge of my radar screen. With a judicious adjustment of the hand controller I tried to enhance the clarity of the blip. I became mentally immersed in the information on the radar screen – to the point, perhaps, that I was too focussed and was slow to appreciate the implications when my radar picture began to display unusual signs.

The hazard was compounded as I put the problem down initially to the dark art of electronic counter measures. Maybe at that point I relaxed my guard a little. Eventually, however, sensory conflicts and illusions started to niggle at my subconscious mind.

Abruptly, I snapped my head away from the radar hood. Reality struck without mercy. Shocked, I hesitated for a moment or two. My flight instruments revealed contradictory data; I had just seconds in which to separate true from false. I suddenly realised that the main artificial horizon, which was linked to the display on the radar screen, was askew compared to the indications on the standby artificial horizon. In the pitch-black conditions I relied entirely on my flight instruments for orientation. By now I was convinced that I needed to ignore the main instrument and to concentrate instead on the small, awkwardly-placed standby artificial horizon. The latter, along with the altimeter, were together trying to scream the full extent of danger.

By this stage the Lightning was in a steep dive with 70 degrees of right bank and the altimeter was winding down below 400 feet as I plummeted towards the sea. At once, I slammed the Lightning's control stick to the left and pulled back to the limit of 6g. The aircraft reacted immediately, although I reckoned that the altimeter 'bottomed-out' at 200 feet. Within seconds, though, I had zoom-climbed the Lightning to an altitude of 5,000 feet. My heartbeat racing, I advised the controller that my aircraft was unserviceable and that I would return to base at once. "That's copied," he said nonchalantly.

I flew back to Akrotiri at a safe altitude and landed without further incident. However, while I completed the necessary paperwork, I was unable to rid my mind of ghosts from the past. During my Hawker Hunter training course at RAF Chivenor, Devon, a colleague had been lost in similar circumstances. Hunters and Lightnings carried no 'black box' data recorders, but the Hunter pilot had crashed not into the sea but into a farmer's field. By piecing together the aircraft's scattered fragments, accident investigators could work out that spatial disorientation had been the root cause of the young pilot's tragic death. As I remembered this, I knew that that night I had been toying with the stuff of disaster.

When, eventually, I finished form-filling, I felt the need to wander outside. Earlier cloud layers had dispersed by now and I could observe a slim, small moon. A mass of stars wheeled up into the sky. I could barely make out the line of distant hills, but I recalled how, at dusk, the last traces of spring sunshine had provided a colourful backdrop to the contours of Mount Olympus. At present, however, all remained dark while I pondered and breathed the cool, unforgiving night air.

CHAPTER 19

A NIGHT TO REMEMBER

ALI McKAY'S NORTH SEA DIP

A bitter, sodden wind swept across the water. I glanced up at the rush of noise as a Lightning flew low across my position. A sharp stab of optimism, however, swiftly subsided as I resumed my baling routine. I could not avoid speculation on the possibility of miscalculation; perhaps I had misread the cockpit information, maybe the whole dire situation had been caused by some terrible error of judgement. Perhaps it was my own fault that I now faced the prospect of hours spent bobbing about in a flimsy dinghy on the surface of the North Sea.

It was exactly eleven fifteen when, on that fateful evening of 26th May 1971, I had taken off in Lightning XS902. It was my second sortie that night in XS902 which had just been returned to our squadron (5[F] Squadron based at RAF Binbrook in Lincolnshire) after major servicing at a specialist maintenance unit. As might be expected, XS902 had gleamed inside and out after its servicing, furthermore the aircraft's radar had seemed to be working particularly well. I was anxious, therefore, to make the most of the opportunity of a second flight in this aircraft to allow me to consolidate low level intercept skills before my forthcoming course to become an intercept weapons instructor.

Now ensconced in my dinghy, I looked up at the night sky and memory stirred. When my boss had summonsed me to announce the news that I'd been selected for that course, I'd felt a thrill of excitement. It had seemed, somehow, a fitting endorsement after the years of hard work needed to take me to that point – years, indeed, that had begun in a somewhat unlikely way. I was a lad of nearly fifteen when I experienced my first small taste of air force life. It was back then when, as a pupil at Inverness Royal Academy in Scotland, I was offered an opportunity to attend a presentation by a Royal Air Force recruitment team. Faced with the alternative of a double lesson in religious instruction, I opted for the RAF presentation. The presentation had started with a black-and-white movie clip of 92 Squadron's 'Blue Diamond' Hawker Hunter aerobatic team. The impact on my nearly-fifteen-year-old psyche was profound; my mind, one might say, was almost blown away.

Enthralled by what I'd seen and heard, at the end of the presentation I spoke with a member of the RAF team. "We're looking for candidates who wish to leave school at the age of fifteen to join the service under our Boy Entrant scheme," he said.

"Will the Boy Entrants become pilots?" I asked ingenuously.

"No, lad," he said, "to become a pilot you'll need to stay on at school, study hard and pass exams."

"Oh."

However, it was the Blue Diamond aerobatic stuff that had fascinated me; that, I said to the man, was what I really wanted. "In that case," he said, "I suggest you join the Inverness Air Training Corps. You'll learn about the service and meet other air-minded types."

After school that day I discussed the issue with my mother. My father had died when I was seven years of age so I'd had to rely on my mother for parental guidance. She was, though, less than enthusiastic about my air force aspirations – unlike three of my best friends at school, all of whom came from the same Inverness council housing estate where I lived with my mother, and all of whom had obtained parental approval to join the RAF under the Boy Entrant scheme. "If you join the Air Training Corps," my mother pointed out to me, "you'll have to leave the scouts."

"I suppose so."

"But you've just been made patrol leader of Peewit Patrol."

"I know."

Despite my mother's reservations, I did indeed sacrifice my position as leader of Peewit Patrol and joined the Air Training Corps instead. It proved, though, to be a good decision. After three years as a member of the Inverness

Air Training Corps, and encouraged by an excellent commanding officer, I was promoted to the rank of cadet flight sergeant, achieved a Gold Award under the Duke of Edinburgh's scheme, passed the necessary educational qualifications at school, gained my private pilot's licence through the RAF's Flying Scholarship programme and last, but by no means least, been offered a place as a flight cadet at the RAF College, Cranwell. In October 1964 I duly took up my place.

It was some four or five years after that when I received my first posting to an operational squadron – 5(F) Squadron as, joy of joys, a Lightning pilot.

Tension was high on 5 Squadron at that time. Aircraft serviceability was poor and there were doubts about the ability to meet commitments, in particular the deployment of the whole squadron to Singapore. Not long after I'd joined the squadron commanding officer was sacked and an interim CO, a man with a reputation for ruthlessness and for getting things done, was appointed. Right at the start of his short period in post, the new CO came up with a novel concept: the hangar doors would be kept locked and personnel not allowed to leave until the required number of serviceable aircraft had been achieved. A man who was an exceptional Lightning pilot and who was concerned with results rather than popularity, the new CO's methods had – surprise, surprise – brought about a dramatic improvement in aircraft serviceability rates.

At the end of his six-month or so stint, the interim CO left the squadron and I was introduced to my third commanding officer. Third time lucky, I thought, when I reflected ruefully that I was still on my first tour. Fortunately, I got on well with the new CO and I was excited when selected as one of six squadron pilots to take part in a NATO air defence competition. The competition had gone well for us, serviceability rates continued to be good and only a month earlier I had been part of a large squadron flypast held to celebrate the fact that we had won the air defence competition.

The fates, however, seldom give us what we wanted in the way that we wanted and now the tables had turned with a vengeance. An hour or so earlier, shortly after my take-off from Binbrook, I'd been climbing through an altitude of around 4,000 feet when I first spotted trouble. A caption that announced 'Fire 1' had illuminated on XS902's warning panel accompanied by a cautionary klaxon in my headset earpieces. At once I cancelled reheat on both engines. As I did this, the 'Reheat 1' caption illuminated – fire in number one engine's reheat zone. My cockpit was suddenly overwhelmed with warning lights and klaxons. The situation did not look good and a glance at the emergencies panel revealed a rare jackpot: Fire 1, Fire 2, Reheat 1, Reheat 2 and a few other indications thrown in for good measure. Without further ado I cried out on the aircraft radio: "*Mayday...Mayday...Mayday...*" My wingman, Flight Lieutenant Merv Fowler, then announced excitedly that the rear of my aircraft was on fire. "I can see white flame," he said, "I suggest you eject."

At this stage I left my number two engine running in cold power (ie without reheat) and XS902, ironically, continued to climb quite smoothly. All around, though, a sickening suspense hung in the air. My brain struggled to come to terms with reality. Despite the fearsome prospects, the comfort of the immediate here-and-now held strong attraction: my cockpit felt cosy and familiar; the cockpit lighting, albeit enhanced by the emergencies panel, seemed perfectly satisfactory; below me the acquainted lights of the town of Grimsby started to disappear behind my Lightning. In many ways, things looked pretty much normal; surely I wouldn't have to abandon this aircraft, this machine newly out of deep maintenance, still shiny, still pristine, and deposit it – and myself – into the dreaded depths of the North Sea?

Suddenly XS902's flight controls started to 'hunt'. Later, I learnt that this was a sign that the control rods had begun to expand and contract in the heat of the fire; it would not be long before the control rods melted and the Lightning would be uncontrollable. My brief period of false solace would come to an abrupt end. Thoughts such as 'this cannot be happening to me' wanted to rush around my head but I was too preoccupied for distractions. I therefore had a final check around the cockpit, tightened my ejection seat straps as much as possible, ensured that the Lightning was pointing out to sea, then called on the aircraft radio that I was ejecting. After that, I reached up to clasp the ejection seat handle above my head. When I pulled the handle, I pulled it hard.

A momentary pause ensued before I heard a bang and felt a jolt as my ejection seat's primary cartridge shot me clear of the doomed Lightning. I was thrust precipitously into a world of weird, whirling activity. Time, vision and perspective became alarmingly confused. I tumbled then felt a sharp pull on my helpless body. When I realised that my continued physical existence appeared reasonably assured, even if it did rely on the parachute canopy blossoming above my head, I experienced a great surge of relief. I was aware of jet engine noise in the vicinity which rapidly developed into a roar as my wingman's Lightning flashed passed my right side. He seemed incredibly close and I could remember yelling absurdly: "Merv! Don't do a turn-back!"

Surreal thoughts started to work through my head as I descended in my parachute. There was a curious calm – a sense of peace after the furious activity up to the point of ejection. Memories of a balmy day, a light breeze and rain in the night, a place where wild flowers bloomed, wanted to prevail over others. The high-tech cockpit with its endless demands and fantastic possibilities seemed rather ridiculous, as if from a by-gone era. I was in the hands of nature now and fantastic possibilities of another kind lay ahead.

Aware that the sea's surface would loom shortly, I unclipped my personal survival pack and lowered it on a lanyard. I'd practised the procedure many times in 'dry drills'. It contained, among other items, my flimsy but vital one-man rubber dinghy. As soon as the pack struck the water I could brace myself for a sea dip within seconds. Abruptly, however, the carefully practised procedures appeared to turn pear shaped when my personal survival pack began to oscillate wildly from side to side like an unsynchronised pendulum. Conscious of the case of another Lightning pilot who, just a year earlier, had died of exposure in the sea having lost his personal survival pack, at once I hauled up the pack and tucked it firmly under my right arm.

As my inevitable sea dip grew ever closer, I fumbled for my Mae West life jacket's beaded operating handle and tugged hard at which the jacket inflated in an instant. The scene below looked fiendishly dark but not so dark as to conceal drifts of spume blown by the wind across wave tops. I attempted to assess the sea swell and general conditions when...*SPLASH!*...one Lightning pilot was deposited with a wallop face first into the North Sea.

I felt myself gasp for breath. A wave rolled over my head (so Lightning pilots couldn't walk on water after all; pity, really). I rotated then squeezed my parachute release box at which the 'chute was whipped away by the wind.

Now I needed to force myself to remain calm, to focus on correct drills. I felt for my personal survival pack's lanyard…where the hell was it? – jeepers – *don't panic – move the fingers along the bottom of the Mae West – locate the fastener – there – haul in the lanyard – hold the pack in the left hand – pull the handle – it works, thank God...the rubber dinghy's inflated – turn the dinghy the right way up – clamber in...easier said than done...my immersion suit's full of water – I'm all arms and legs – place the canopy over the head – blow some puffs of air into the canopy and into the dinghy floor – retrieve the personal survival pack – place it under the knees – check that the sea drogue's deployed…*

Working away like an automaton, I carried out the drills just as I been required to perform them in so many practice sessions. These sessions may have been regarded at the time as boring but they undoubtedly helped to save my life.

Essential tasks, though, remained. After protection, the next priority...location. Hurriedly, I extracted the SARBE (search and rescue beacon equipment) location device from a pocket, then pulled a tag to erect the aerial and switch on the beacon. I held the SARBE close to my ear to listen for a 'mewing' sound; this confirmed that the transmitter was working and that the emergency signal should be picked up by rescue services. I made sure that my McMurdo light was working then re-checked around my 'cockpit': *sea drogue deployed...SARBE activated...McMurdo light on...canopy inflated...dinghy floor inflated.* Excellent, I thought, everything's shipshape... should have joined the bloody navy.

Now tossed by the swell, it was not long before my dinghy began to fill with water. As the effect of adrenaline within my system began to subside, I realised that I was cold and wet; seawater had penetrated my immersion suit through the neck seal which had been torn during the ejection sequence. The tiny dinghy's confused motion started to make me feel seasick and my teeth began to chatter with the numbing cold. One moment a wave hoisted me skywards until, after a fleeting hesitation, the dinghy plunged down again. I struggled to use the rubber bailer but water persisted to flood into my dinghy at an ever-faster rate. At length, faced with a losing battle, I decided to investigate the contents of my personal survival pack; among other things, I could remind myself of the pyrotechnics available to reveal my position if and when the rescue services arrived.

As I reflected on my situation I could not avoid disagreeable doubts. Perhaps the Whirlwind rescue helicopters from Leconfield would not operate at night; I couldn't really remember about this, but reckoned that I might be faced with a long wait, a protracted and tortuous night. I worried endlessly about the events leading up to my ejection. Perhaps I had been wrong about the cockpit indications. Maybe I'd made a fearful error of judgement. I worried, too, about my wife Coreen and what she'd been told. A few months ago, Coreen, in company with the station padre, the medical officer, the squadron commanding officer and his wife, had gone to comfort the wife of a USAF exchange officer who was missing after an accident following a low level interception at night. I speculated on whether a similar team was currently congregated at my house.

An eerie wind, as it blew from the springtime points of the weather, hardly helped to settle my uneasiness. In this clash of reality with unreality I felt at once the irony which tried to mock me and would not let me be. I wanted to hit out at some illusory creature – a hateful wretch that tried to scoff...'I have no fear of you,' it appeared to say, 'your violence will avail you nothing. Fight or otherwise, you are doomed.' My facial expression must have hardened. Behind me I could picture my colleagues, my fellow squadron pilots, impassive, silent, watchful. I seemed to see a figure of myself, drawn and repelled.

I stared at distant clouds as if they possessed preternatural powers that could turn the wheel of memory. Stimulated, perhaps, by a form of hallucination, haunting recollections danced within my imagination. As if in sympathy with the sea's movement, one moment I felt within myself the power to rise to the greatest heights until pride suffered the severest of shocks when the dinghy plummeted at which, under nature's cruel command, all little superficial vanities and egotisms fell away.

Still afflicted by seasickness, I decided to rummage in my personal survival pack again. I came across a solar still – a low-tech device that produced distilled water when heated by the rays of the sun. Sun? At night over the North Sea? I wanted to let out a loud guffaw, shrug my shoulders which, under different circumstances, might have started to shake with laughter. With a suitable adjustment of the position of the McMurdo light, at least I could read the solar still's operating instructions which were quite complex. This would occupy my mind and take my thoughts away from feeling seasick. Suddenly, just as I was settling in to my 'book at bedtime', I heard a roar as a Lightning flew low overhead. My morale soared and a sense of dreadful loneliness eased when I realised that my wingman must have picked up the signal from my SARBE beacon and homed onto my position.

For the next few hours, this informal patrol was maintained by squadron colleagues. My flight commander, when he'd heard that my wingman had detected a SARBE signal, had organised a rota of Lightnings to overfly my position at regular intervals – a brilliant and solicitous touch which helped to keep up my spirits during the ordeal. After some hours the Lightning patrol system ended and instead of jet engine noise I could hear the unmistakeable drone of an Avro Shackleton aircraft. The heavy brigade are here at last, I thought. With the Shackleton flying at low level I learned later that the Lightning patrol had been called off so as not to interfere with search and rescue operations.

My troubles, however, were not over yet. In a rhythmic, automatic routine I persisted with baling out seawater – a monotony which added to my sense of bewilderment, of exhaustion, of anxiety. My head spun giddily; a ringing in the ears caused thought processes to come and go far more rapidly than usual. I was aware of flares being fired by the Shackleton but convinced myself that the helicopter probably wouldn't make it until morning.

The noise, when I first heard it, seemed to appear from nowhere. It came in the middle of what I was thinking and made me stop short as I felt the implications flow into my brain and I kept very still and let the sound come and keep on coming and almost before I knew what was happening I had the whole thing, the whole incredible prospect, the magnificent reality that I knew that I wasn't, after all, destined to die this night.

I couldn't see anything for a while but at length, as the clamour wafted and wavered within the howl of the wind to develop gradually into the familiar clatter of a helicopter, I felt a feeling such as I have never known before or since. My heart leapt; I experienced a curious, choking emotion, a poignant hopefulness as if a protective arm had clasped my shoulders.

This, however, was not the time for reverie. I turned to look behind me as the whip of helicopter blades came closer. The sight astonished me. Within the glare of flashlights that probed the dark, I could spot a spectral shape which, like some supernatural waterskier, was crashing through the waves towards my position. The spectacle was unreal. The apparition, which I suddenly realised was a helicopter winchman, bore down on me with fluorescent froth churning below his feet. Later, I learnt that the helicopter pilot was prohibited from hovering at night in these conditions. Ever resourceful and courageous, the helicopter crew nonetheless had decided to attempt rescue by scooping me up 'on the run'. The helicopter crewman consequently hit me at fairly high speed. A bit of a grab and a wrestle ensued before he managed eventually to attach me to a double strop. The crewman then used a hack-knife to cut me free from the dinghy and within moments we were both on our way up to the Whirlwind's cabin as the helicopter winch operator hauled us aboard.

The flight back to Binbrook did not take long. I'd been in the sea for some four hours and the helicopter crew kept me lying on my back until the station medical officer had checked me over. When he arrived, the medical officer was accompanied by a squadron pilot. "Please state your name and address," said the medical officer. I told him, presumably to his satisfaction, for the medical officer then gave my squadron colleague permission to hand over a bottle of whisky. We retired to the squadron crew room where I was told to don a fluffy 'bunny suit' which, together with a large dram of whisky, helped to restore my body core temperature. I tried to tackle some of the inescapable paperwork but by about 6.30am, with signs of sunrise on the horizon, I decided to head for home where I knew that my wife Coreen would be anxious to hear about what had been going on.

When I reached my married quarter I noticed that the window curtains were drawn and that all seemed quiet. I let myself in to the house and everything continued to seem quiet. I felt a little surprised, hurt even, at the lack of a welcoming committee. "Oh well," I thought philosophically, "life goes on, I suppose." The sight of our personal possessions, though, suddenly made me feel quite emotional. In a flash of memory there came an image of what I'd been through. Unlike some who'd ejected from aeroplanes, I'd survived the ordeal and the thought seemed to prompt a surge of *joie de vivre*. "I'm home," I shouted while pouring myself a further large dram of whisky, selecting an Elton John number on our Hi-Fi set and turning up the volume.

It was as I hunted around for ingredients to make up a celebratory gin and tonic for Coreen that she walked into the room. I had no gift for epigram or brilliant repartee at that moment; I might even have stood there guiltily, jaw ajar as she cried with great rapidity, if somewhat inarticulately, comments about selfish individuals who came in late to make such a ridiculous racket that it disturbed everyone else especially when that person knew perfectly well that an early start for his wife's nursing job today of all days when a full shift was involved and which therefore necessitated a good night's rest and the last straw was…

"Why are you wearing that peculiar fluffy suit?" she interrupted her rant. My normally quiet, patient and understanding wife now stood and stared at me. Our eyes for the first time really met. In a small but significant way, out of obscurity came a distant, slight something that stooped and looked out at me for a mere instant of time which seemed of intolerable protraction. In an involuntary gesture I blinked and shook my head. "My God," she went on, "something's happened, hasn't it?"

"A bit of a tarradiddle," I found my voice.

"Go on…"

My blood was still chilled, my limbs persisted to feel weighted, there were shadows that frolicked before my eyes as I told her the whole sorry saga which came tumbling out in terse, emotional bursts.

Later, I learnt that the flight commander, when he knew that my SARBE signal had been picked up, had decided that I was probably still alive and that the best plan, therefore, would be to allow Coreen a good night's rest instead of a 'doom-watch committee' hanging around in our married quarter through the night. He had to make a difficult – well nigh impossible – decision which, with the benefit of hindsight, probably turned out to be the right one.

It was later in the day, too, that I learnt that the doctors, worried about damage to my spine, insisted that I was taken without delay for hospital treatment. At RAF Nocton Hall Hospital I was fitted with a neck brace and made to lie flat on my back, a process that went on for several weeks and caused me considerable frustration. Frustration turned to anguish when the medics told me that I was unlikely to fly ejection seat-equipped aircraft again. At length, however, after several weeks at Nocton Hall followed by a few months at the rehabilitation centre at RAF Headley Court, I won my battle to regain a medical category which included ejection seat-equipped aircraft. In mid-November 1971, having been grounded for some six months, I had a thirty-minute check-ride in the squadron's two-seat Lightning T5. Over the next few days I flew various intercept sorties in single-seat F6 Lightnings and on the sixth day I flew an instrument rating test with Flight Lieutenant Merv Fowler, my wingman on the night of the ejection. I was then declared combat ready and took part in an air defence exercise based at RAF Lossiemouth. The following April I began my delayed intercept weapons instructor's course.

After 5 Squadron I was posted to another Lightning squadron, 92 (East India) Squadron in Germany, before I converted to the F4 Phantom. I served on the F4 operational conversion unit at RAF Coningsby, on 23(F) Squadron as a squadron leader qualified weapons instructor, on 92 Squadron (by then equipped with the F4 Phantom) as a flight commander and I spent eighteen months as a member of the Strike Command tactical evaluation team. My last tour on Phantoms was as officer commanding 56(F) Squadron at RAF Wattisham at the end of which I was sent to the Falklands for five months. My last tour in the service was as station commander at RAF Wildenrath in Germany. I decided at that point to leave the Royal Air Force but as I had no desire to fly airliners I applied for a senior management training scheme with the John Lewis Partnership. I felt very fortunate to be selected and within a year I was given a principal director position when I became the retail and operations director for Waitrose and a member of the Waitrose board. After eleven years in that position I moved to a corporate post and joined the main partnership board. For my last two years in the partnership I took up the role of deputy chairman.

On reflection, as my mother would have pointed out, "Alastair you have been a very lucky boy". A key theme in both of my careers has been to find ways to 'get the job done' and to get it done well. There were times, however, when I was in the John Lewis boardroom for a meeting that I would look around at my colleagues and wonder whether they had ever gone through anything like the same levels of excitement, fear and drama which I had experienced. And if, in a lightning flash of memory, there came a picture before the throw-back faded under the present, almost inevitably this would have involved my experiences on that 'night to remember'.

CHAPTER 20

IT'S OVER

RICHARD PIKE RECALLS A TURBULENT TIME

There were quick footsteps to the door before the fire officer burst in. As he swished in he said: "They're bonkers, the lot of them."

"Yes, yes," said someone indulgently.

"Hmmm," he said.

The fire chief now stormed about smacking his fist into his palm and exclaiming: "damn, damn, damn", until suddenly he seemed to be struck with some good ideas. The pilots, quietly glad, I suspected, to have the operations room's tense atmosphere eased by our unconventional fire officer, played along with his distraction.

"I tell you they're mad – off their trollies," said the fire officer. "And by the way," he added petulantly, "it's entirely due to you lot that my poor firemen are kept so busy anyway."

I was not to know, of course, quite how prophetic his words were about to prove. In any case, promptly interrupted by the operations officer's call "*four Lightnings to cockpit readiness...get going everyone*", the interlude had to be put swiftly behind us. As we pilots started to run to our aircraft, groundcrews raced ahead of us. "Good luck, lads..." the fire officer's voice trailed behind us.

In addition to the three other Lightning pilots, I ran in company with a Danish lieutenant, a Lockheed F104 Starfighter pilot. The lieutenant would be

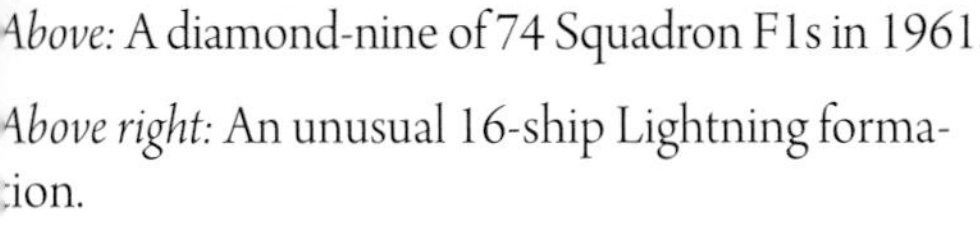

Above: A diamond-nine of 74 Squadron F1s in 1961.

Above right: An unusual 16-ship Lightning formation.

Right: Pilots preparing for a high-altitude flight with the infamous Taylor helmets on.

Below: 56 Squadron T5 approaching touchdown.

Top: Line up of 11(F) Squadron F6s.

Inset: 74 Squadron F6 XR768 complete with over-wing tanks and airbrakes out.

Bottom: A 111(F) Squadron Lightning at Akrotiri.

'op: 56 Squadron T5 at slow speed.

Aiddle left: Flight Lieutenant Don Brown taking off n a 74(F) Squadron F3 from RAF Leuchars, Scot-
ınd.

Middle right: T4 XM973 which first flew in May 1961.

Above: Prototype T4 XL628 which was abandoned by English Electric test pilot, Johnny Squier on 1 October 1959 over the Irish Sea.

Lightning Mk 6 fighters of 5 Squadron in line abreast.

my passenger in the two-seat T4 Lightning trainer (XM991) allocated to me for the exercise. As 19(F) Squadron's instrument rating examiner I was used to flying the T4 regularly and deemed, therefore, as suitable to take up our guest. A member of a Danish air force squadron, he would gain first-hand knowledge of our squadron's *modus operandi*. This, the theory went, would help to enhance a common bond within NATO's members. Like all good theories, however, it was the exception that proved the rule, and today we were about to stretch a rule or two.

Assisted by two ground crewmen, we strapped in to our respective ejection seats hastily. When ready, the ground crewmen removed and stowed our seat safety pins, stepped down the ladders on each side of the cockpit, removed the ladders, then stood, arms folded, by a pre-positioned fire extinguisher. All of us would now endure a period of waiting until the Lightnings were ordered airborne by the controller. The aircraft, parked near the squadron buildings at RAF Gütersloh in Germany, overlooked a cavernous hangar with equipment and aircraft components scattered across oil-spattered, roughened floors. Hidden from our present view were staff in offices at the back of the hangar who continued, no doubt, with necessary administrative routines despite the hectic flying activity outside. Unlike the Battle Flight set-up at Gütersloh, with two armed Lightnings in a special hangar at the end of the runway, we would have some distance to taxy to the take-off point. Even so, when ordered to scramble, our slick, well-honed procedures invariably ensured that we'd be airborne well before five minutes had elapsed.

Although altogether different nowadays, back then in the late 1960s RAF Gütersloh held a unique position. To the east, just a few minutes' flying time in a Lightning, lay the iniquitous 'Iron Curtain', more correctly known as the Inner German Border, that stretched for nine hundred miles or so to separate the West from the East. This man-made obscenity comprised massive rolls of barbed wire, special dog runs, minefields, floodlights, carefully combed sandy strips, anti-vehicle ditches, automatic alarms, booby traps and a series of tall watchtowers manned by some 50,000 armed guards. Unless ordered to do so, we were not allowed to enter a so-called buffer zone, let alone cross the border itself. Border infringements by land or air could lead to big trouble – ultimately World War Three could be triggered.

"What's this?" The Danish lieutenant pointed with one finger. I glanced at him before replying. He had a pale, wide-open face; his eyes were bright and dark. His English was near-perfect with just a trace of accent. When, earlier, we had talked in the mess he'd described how his hazy schoolboy dream to become a pilot had put him in a world he had not really anticipated – one that stretched minds, offered high satisfaction, an arcane transcendence to the reality of becoming an operational fighter pilot.

"That's the tail 'chute operating handle," I said in reply to his question.

"Oh, yes." He paused before going on jauntily: "Seems we're to be kept waiting for a while."

"We're at the controller's beck and call."

"Huh," he snorted. "Controllers!" This remark was prompted, I supposed, by an earlier conversation when we'd discussed local procedures for ground controlled approaches to landing, otherwise known as GCA.

"I was flying with one of our squadron pilots in the T4 Lightning the other day," I told him, "when the talk-down controller sounded bored so we decided to hot things up a bit."

"I understand," he said even though it was apparent that he did not understand.

"We were settled at normal airspeed for a GCA," I went on to explain, "when – after mutual head nods – the other pilot and I decided to raise the flaps and the undercarriage before applying a burst of reheat."

The lieutenant started to grin as comprehension dawned.

"As our airspeed increased, so did the pace of the controller's talk-down patter. It was quite impressive, really. What you might term an exponential rate of talk-down velocity. Until, that is, the controller suddenly realised what was going on and stopped talking altogether."

"What happened next?"

"The bloody controller had a sense of humour failure, that's what happened. He complained to our wing commander. As a consequence, the other pilot and I were rostered for extra Battle Flight duties – worthy but dull penance."

"*...maintain cockpit readiness...*" the current controller's voice crackled through our headsets.

"A bit longer to wait," I said to the lieutenant. He nodded. I checked my watch and glanced at the other pilots, all experienced Lightning men. Postings to the Lightning force in Germany tended to be reserved for older hands – non-wet-behind-the-ears types who were considered suitable for operations close to the Iron Curtain. We all sat expectantly in our cockpits, anxious for proceedings to start. Earlier, we had been briefed that the other Lightnings would move ahead of mine when the scramble order came; the T4, it was decided, should act as Tailend Charlie.

The Danish lieutenant began to fiddle with his oxygen mask. "You okay?" I asked him. He gave a thumbs-up sign but said nothing. Perhaps the suspense was getting to him. A passenger flight in a Lightning was a rare treat; doubtless he had looked forward to this moment but the waiting around was not good. It could get on the nerves.

Suddenly the controller's voice piped up again "*...as briefed, scramble...*" and at once a burst of activity could be observed around all four Lightnings. Circling motions with fingers were followed by the shrill *wheeee* sound of starter motors. When all engines were turning and burning, groundcrews then scurried about to detach external power units and remove wheel chocks. In nearly no time at all the Lightnings were taxying out in the planned order for take-off.

"*Clear for immediate take-off*," announced the controller, who sounded harassed. As we approached the take-off point, the lead Lightning moved directly onto the runway. Without delay, he opened up his throttles after which, with intervals of just a few seconds, the others followed in sequence. As I was last in the stream take-off I had to be wary of wake turbulence but a reasonable crosswind on that September day reduced the hazard. When I selected full cold power, a roar from the twin Rolls-Royce Avon engines was accompanied by a surge of acceleration. After a short delay I rocked the twin throttles outboard then pushed them forward to the full reheat position. A momentary pause ensued, as if the engines were thinking about what to do next, until a further roar and a powerful punch in the back confirmed that both engines' reheat systems had kicked in.

I monitored the airspeed as we progressed and my peripheral vision picked up a blur of runway on each side as we accelerated. At the appropriate airspeed I raised the nosewheel and very shortly after that the mainwheels left the runway surface. Ahead, the other Lightnings had started to turn and I watched them carefully as I felt for the undercarriage operating button. Having raised the undercarriage and completed other after take-off checks, I continued to follow the Lightnings ahead. We were climbing through around 3,000 feet when, quite abruptly, the focus of my attention had to flick from outside to inside the cockpit. A cautionary klaxon in my headset and a swift check of the aircraft warning panel revealed that we had suffered a 'Fire 2' – fire in number two engine (the top engine).

At once, I throttled back the affected engine and carried out emergency drills. These included a 'PAN' emergency call on the radio which caused the harassed controller to sound even more harassed. I turned back towards the airfield and it was then, as I glanced at my passenger, that I suddenly saw him reach for his ejection seat handle. "No!" I cried, "don't touch that. We've had an engine fire but it's under control...I'll have you down in no time at all." Regretfully, his grasp of the English language, near-perfect when conditions were calm, seemed to falter under pressure. Perhaps I had spoken too rapidly, I didn't know, but whatever the cause he appeared not to understand. I was tempted to reach across and physically remove his hands from the ejection seat handle but this action could be fraught with danger; any form of struggle might set off the ejection seat. Besides which, cross-cockpit touching can be liable to inappropriate interpretation.

I decided, therefore, to attempt a further verbal appeal: "Don't worry," I said as soothingly as possible, "we'll land safely, very soon." I tried to keep the language simple. My passenger, though, stared straight ahead as if frozen with fear. His hands still grasped the ejection seat handle and I was uncertain whether he had understood me. Meanwhile, I had to concentrate on the emergency landing. Precipitate action by my passenger was a worrying possibility, nonetheless my priority was to carry out a safe landing – hopefully with him still on board.

As I turned downwind, then onto finals, I needed even greater than normal vigilance. As well as routine procedures, I had to check regularly behind me to search for signs of smoke or fire. I felt, too, the need to glance frequently at my passenger in order to monitor the tightness of his grip on his ejection seat handle. If he pulled the handle – if he actually ejected himself from the Lightning – the perspex canopy would be ejected too and I would have to rely on a small area of fixed windshield for protection from winds of 200 knots or so.

For the landing itself, I aimed for a firm touchdown as near to the runway threshold as possible; too firm, perhaps, for the lieutenant whose angst clearly remained unassuaged. When, at last, we reached the end of the landing run, I manoeuvred the Lightning clear of the runway and shut down the good engine. Finally he appeared willing to release his grip on the handle.

Fire crews now raced up to the Lightning and parked in a circle around us. Firemen ran up to assist with cockpit evacuation, though I noted the lack of their fire officer's presence. I assumed that he was too busy dreaming up quirky ideas to bother with mundane matters like extinguishing fires. His men then drove the lieutenant and myself to the squadron set-up during which journey I raised the issue of the ejection seat handle. To my surprise, the lieutenant seemed unrepentant. He stressed that an engine fire in one of his squadron's single-engined F104 Starfighters would almost inevitably have involved an ejection. I had to admit that he had a point.

When the fire truck had dropped us off at the squadron buildings, the lieutenant and I made our way upstairs to the operations room. As we walked in,

I noted that the fire officer's bulky frame had been replaced by a rather different one: a slip-of-a-lass secretary employed by the squadron on a part-time basis. The pilots all had a soft spot for her – impulsive, pretty, mercurial and mischievous as she was. One pilot in particular had become close to her although the relationship appeared to have struck a rocky patch of late. In the officers' mess, as our tame squadron suitor sat at the bar, his increasing alcohol consumption would fuel heartfelt talk of his woes although the mess bar, with its sometimes nervy bonhomie, could be an unsuitable place to delve into the curious countries of the heart.

All of this, of course, was unknown to our Danish guest as we entered the ops room that day. In addition to normal post-flight paperwork, I had forms to fill in and questions to answer about our emergency. As I did so, I sensed, as usual, the necessary swift but subtle mental switch needed post-flight; the immediacy of airborne issues and consequent intense concentration soon became diluted as earthly matters intervened.

For one thing, I could not avoid reflections on my recent news. Just a few days ago the squadron boss had summoned me to his office to announce that I had been posted. "After five years of Lightning flying on three different squadrons," he'd said, "you've done well." A small but ominous hesitation had followed. "However, the powers-that-be feel that a ground tour will be in your best interests at this stage of your career." Another hesitation, then he had blurted out: "You've been posted to Headquarters 11 Group."

Later, my boss, with whom I got on well, had described with amusement my astonished reaction – so great, he'd said, that my eyebrows had practically reached the back of my head. At the time, though, the news had led to an awkward hush. It was surely crazy, I thought, to take an operational pilot at the peak of his abilities and place him in some obscure back office. What the hell was the point of that? I had joined the service to fly aircraft not to sit at a desk. It was bonkers, like that fire chief. As a simple soul

Sketch by Richard Pike of 19 Squadron Lightning.

(some might say), I had developed from a young age a fascination for – and a love of – flying. At the RAF College, Cranwell I had been awarded the Dickson Trophy and Michael Hill Memorial Prize for flying, and now I had scant desire to 'fly' a desk. When, eventually, I spoke I kept my voice steady even though there was rage within me: "A ground tour, sir?" the words dropped down my throat like a swallowed sweet.

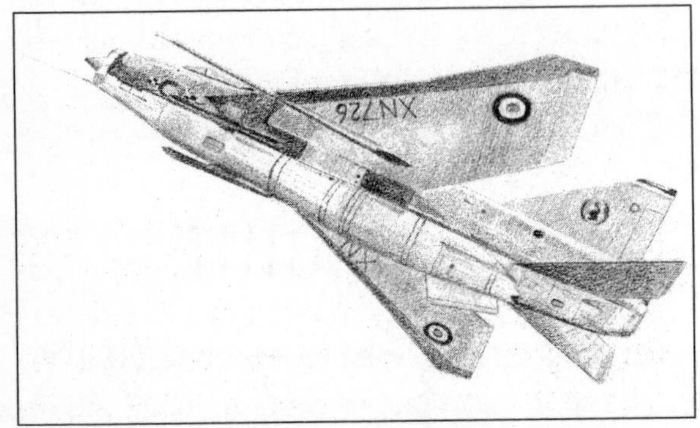

19 Squadron Lightning.

"Yes", the wing commander's eyes studied me carefully, "a ground tour". He had smiled gently then, as if remembering a half-forgotten friend, but there was a trace of troubled conscience in that smile.

"Oh well," I said dully, "life's full of surprises, I suppose."

Just now, however, with the paperwork completed, I invited the Danish lieutenant along to the pilots' crew room. "You've earned yourself a coffee," I said. "Sorry your flight was such a short one." He shrugged as if to say, '*c'est la vie*'.

In the crew room we joined a few other pilots, one of whom was our tame squadron suitor in a morose mood. From the drift of conversation I realised that he was in trouble again. An aura of hurt was palpable; his voice had become heavy. He kept his head low and I could hardly see his eyes but I reckoned that I caught a glint of tears. He mumbled some comment and in the silence that followed I could hear a voice chatting on the phone and the beat of music in the background – the nostalgic melody of 'up, up and away in my beautiful balloon'. Then the door clicked as someone distributing mail slipped into the room. When I glanced at the slip-of-a-lass newcomer – so pretty, so mercurial – I noticed that she was wearing a special dress and that she had taken trouble to make-up her face. No amount of facial cosmetics, though, could hide the despondent, haunted look that told us how empty she felt inside.

"It's over," I thought.

The irony suddenly struck. It was over for me too; my Lightning days were ending; it was final.

TECHNICAL ANNEX

A TRIBUTE TO ROBBIE –

SQUADRON LEADER J C 'ROBBIE' CAMERON

RAF Nicosia, October 1968. Terry Davies is far right.

BY AIR COMMODORE T C DAVIES CENG FIET FRAES

I was always intrigued by his smoker's pipe. Clearly it was an engineering officer's pipe: well-made, well-worn and held together with araldite glue and electrical insulation tape. He was forever tamping it down or digging into it with a screwdriver or feeler gauge or one of those multi-purpose tools that all pipe smokers seem to play with. This time he took a long puff and said with a smile: "I have come to a momentous decision young Terence." I awaited the response with interest. Throughout the two years I had been his deputy, I had learned to respect the views, advice and counsel of this hands-on, experienced and knowledgeable senior engineering officer who sat opposite me in the cramped and shabby office we shared. "I could never work for a company that made the Lightning," he said. I smiled and nodded; I knew exactly what he meant. Every day, like all Lightning SEngOs, he shouldered the not inconsiderable responsibility of ensuring that there were enough serviceable aircraft to meet the squadron commander's operational and training requirements. Being a Lightning engineer was tough! He had already decided to leave the RAF at a career break point that would enable him to offer a civilian employer another 20 years or so of productive work. But enough was enough; the daily battle of trying to keep Lightning Mark 3 fighters serviceable had left its mark. The manufacturer of the RAF's foremost fighter aircraft would not figure in the future work plans of my boss and mentor.

The fundamental problem was that the Lightning had never been designed to enter squadron service and thus presented a considerable challenge to even the most accomplished maintenance engineer. The Lightning was essentially the result of a research project conceived in 1948 which had spawned an aircraft with unique design and phenomenal performance. But no matter how the designers tinkered with the shape and layout, the basic problem from a maintainer's point of view was that the airframe was wrapped around two powerful engines one mounted above the other. As a consequence, system components had to be stuffed into whatever space was available. More significantly, the hydraulic and fuel plumbing ran alongside the engines and jet pipes. This resulted in a number of serious problems. Firstly and most significantly, a fluid leak from any of the various joints, unions and connections usually meant a fire in a confined area packed with flight critical components – including the rods which connected the pilot's controls to the flying surfaces. Secondly, to get at many of the components for repair, replacement or modification invariably meant the time-consuming removal of major items such as external fuel tanks, engine hatches, engines, jet pipes, and weapon packs. This led directly to two other problems. Every disconnection and reconnection of a major item for access increased the risk of introducing other potentially more serious faults. In turn, this work resulted in a large number of inspections and examinations, including independent checks of safety critical items and full functional tests of every system disturbed to gain access to the faulty equipment. Thus the repair of a small component, which would take only a few hours to rectify on a workbench, often took days to fix, including the not inconsiderable cost of many extra hours of inspection.

Lightning maintenance costs, like all fighter aircraft before or since, were notoriously difficult to calculate because of the many variables involved (eg modification states, manpower levels and the age of the aircraft) and most engineers had their own figures. I used to reckon that around 500 manhours per flying hour was a pretty reasonable estimate for a Lightning F Mk 3 squadron. Some experts refer to the poor reliability of the earlier marks of Lightning and in the early days of its operations there was considerable concern over the support costs of the aircraft. Over the years, though, a large number of reliability modifications improved the situation significantly. For example, the introduction of the brushless AC electrical system resulted in the dramatic improvement of AC system failures. It is quite likely that for the very early marks of Lightning the maintenance hours could well have been much greater than 500 per flying hour.

Possible improvements to the Lightning's problem of fuel shortage were investigated. For instance, some Lightning books refer to a proposal to fit the flaps with integral fuel tanks. The proposal was evidently linked to a possible requirement to fit a rocket booster pack in place of the ventral tank to give an added boost to aircraft performance at high altitudes; fuel in the flaps would compensate for the deletion of the ventral tank. The rocket booster pack, however, did not get the go-ahead and so, to the best of my knowledge, the flaps were never used to carry fuel. Another possibility might have been to place fuel in the wing leading edges but as far as I know this idea was not progressed. Amongst other matters, such a plan would have been a major technical headache if implemented because the leading edges contained a number of key items, including the control runs to the ailerons. Some books refer to a possible navy variant of the Lightning, but this would have necessitated a completely redesigned wing for carrier operations. If it had happened, such a variant would have contained more fuel than the RAF version.

The designers did what they could to ease the maintainer's task. The aircraft was pock-marked with access panels and every squadron had its own contortionist who could insert his arms up to his armpits in the bowels of the aircraft with tools tied to his wrists and somehow disconnect, remove, replace, reconnect and often wire-lock a component by feel only. The RAF also did their bit to help. A maintenance policy was evolved to take advantage of the many opportunities when major items such as engines were removed solely for access to enable routine servicing to be done. This was called opportunity servicing, not to be confused with out-of-phase maintenance which covered many items such as ejection seat cartridges and aircraft batteries which had to be replaced on a calendar rather than a flying hour basis.

To compound the engineering problems, 29 (Fighter) Squadron – the last Lightning squadron to be formed (in 1967) – was provided not with new aircraft but with F Mk 3 aircraft handed over from squadrons converting to the newest variant straight from the factory, the F Mk 6. This resulted in more problems: the higher defect rate of older aircraft and engines which had already been in service for many years; the deeper and longer scheduled servicing task of aircraft and engines which had already flown many hours; and last but not least, a very heavy modification workload not faced by the F Mk 6 squadrons with their new aircraft built to the latest modification standard. We had one brand new aircraft, the two-seat XV 328 'Zulu', christened Zebedee by the groundcrew, which had only two hours on the clock when it was delivered to 29 Squadron. Zulu went through its scheduled servicing cycle like a well mannered lady with very few minor defects.

29 (F) Squadron Lightning T5 'Zulu' at RAF Wattisham, October 1967.

The maintenance problems were compounded by other issues. A chronic spares shortage meant that 'cannibalisation' was widespread. Every squadron had its own 'hangar queen', an aircraft usually on long term repair which was robbed – often to a ridiculous extent. Whilst disguising spares shortages, robbing also meant that the task took twice as long because two components had to be removed and refitted: the unserviceable item and the cannibalised replacement. Again, extra valuable manhours had to be spent on system integrity tests, inspections and independent checks of the two disguised systems.

'hen there were the fuel leaks. The Lightning's thin, aerodynamically efficient ving meant that fuel bags took up too much space so fuel was able to leak, eep and drip from any joint in the wing structure which was inadequately aled – and there were many. Even copious amounts of a sealant called PRC ould not stop all the leaks. Also, there were a large number of vents which ere designed to dump fuel overboard as it heated and expanded. As a result, e hangar floor and the concrete area opposite the squadron hangar, known the pan from which the aircraft were operated, became slippery and treachous. In their wisdom, the RAF provided the groundcrew with shoes with ditly moulded rubber soles which acted like ice skates when in contact with l. One night I was stepping off the wing on to the cockpit access ladder en I slipped and fell over the leading edge head down towards the concrete pan. Fortunately I was able to grab the air-to-air refuelling probe which protruded from beneath the port wing.

Unlike the newer Mark 6 aircraft equipped with the much larger ventral fuel pack, the Mark 3 aircraft of 29 Squadron were fitted with the smaller ventral tank which meant a very short sortie, especially if a lot of reheat was used for the attack profile. It always seemed to me that as soon as the aircraft was launched it was back again! The typical sortie rate for a Mk 3 Lightning was about 45 minutes, which is why the pilots often wanted tanker sorties. During one night shift I calculated that every landing resulted in an average of 2.4 defects – which is why the engineers also liked tanker sorties! In 1968, we lost the Dacre trophy (awarded to the most efficient squadron) because although we had the highest number of sorties in 11 (Fighter) Group that year, we didn't generate the most flying hours which was one of the criteria used to assess performance for the trophy.

Manpower, or rather the lack of it, was always a headache. Lightning squadrons were provided with manpower for 'an extended flying day' which was usually interpreted differently by individual squadron commanders. On 29 Squadron the day started at 0700 hours when, after the previous night's flying programme, the line crew would tow whatever serviceable aircraft were available from the hangar to the pan, then prepare them for flight. The working day ended after night flying, usually at 0200 hours when the night shift had recovered sufficient serviceable aircraft for the following day's flying; ideally a minimum of four aircraft. The day and night shift patterns were regularly disrupted by the many short-notice exercises which meant that the groundcrew often went straight to a 12 hours 'on' and 'off' shift arrangement with the unlucky ones often working 20 or more hours at a stretch.

As if we didn't have enough on our hands, every Lightning squadron seemed to be deluged on a weekly basis with instructions, directives, orders, missives and requests from higher authorities and formations. The most pressing of these were the preliminary warning instructions which usually gave notice of considerable work to follow. They were often triggered by a serious defect signal from one of the Lightning units where a dangerous fault had been discovered. These instructions, which usually arrived on a Friday morning and often meant unplanned overtime during the weekend, regularly threw the maintenance plan into disarray.

The engineering management team comprised just two commissioned engineering officers: a senior engineering officer and his junior – often a first tourist like me straight out of Cranwell. We were supported by one warrant

56(F) Squadron night-time operational turn round in Cyprus.

officer and two flight sergeants to cover day and night shifts, leave, sickness and courses. In those days, because of manpower shortages, a squadron never had its full complement of tradesmen and, like all RAF units, also had to bear the many and often lengthy absences for training. The situation was alleviated only by having more SNCOs in lieu of the junior ranks to which we were ordinarily entitled. This was because of the then-policy of promotion to the producer/supervisor ranks of corporal, sergeant and chief technician by time as well as capability. The NCOs were the backbone of the squadron and without their training, professionalism and good humour the engineering task would have been impossible.

In addition to the high standard of NCOs, each Lightning squadron was well served by some outstanding young technicians and mechanics who regularly performed miracles, often under very difficult conditions and in all weathers. The propulsion mechanics who carried out after-flight inspections of the engines deserve a special mention. On a daily basis they had to squeeze past the radar 'bullet' into the aircraft intake, crawl under the bulge of the cockpit floor and climb up over the bifurcated duct to inspect the turbine blades of the top (No 2) engine located half way along the fuselage deep in the bowels of the aircraft – a gloomy, eerie and claustrophobic experience, especially at night. They then had to exercise their engineering judgement and decide if any turbine blade damage was within or outside the technical limits of acceptability.

The task was made even more unpleasant if the aircraft had flown through a flock of birds and the smell of burnt carcasses had begun to drift forward into the intake from the heat-soaked engines.

As the closest Lightning unit to the Ministry of Defence in London as well as Command and Group Headquarters, members of 29 Squadron, based at Wattisham in Suffolk, had more than their fair share of important visitors. In addition to being a diversion from routine work, the visits gave us an opportunity to show how good we were at operational turn rounds (OTRs). As part of our operational task we had to demonstrate our proficiency at refuelling and re-arming aircraft straight after a combat sortie so that the pilot could return to the fight, usually within five to seven minutes. As soon as the aircraft taxied in and the engines were shut down, the OTR team would swarm over the aircraft and simultaneously carry out a number of tasks. These included: connecting the telebrief cable to the aircraft so that the pilot could receive his scramble instructions straight from the fighter controller; fitting two Red Top or Firestreak missiles; refilling the engine starter tank with isopropyl nitrate fuel known as Avpin; fitting a replacement brake parachute and refuelling the aircraft which was the longest task. Meanwhile, the pilot would remain in the cockpit and be debriefed on the previous sortie by the intelligence officer and briefed on the next mission. As soon as the area around the aircraft was safe, the aircraft marshaller would give a thumbs-up to the pilot to signify that the OTR was completed and he was clear to start engines. Our record time for an OTR from engine shut down to engine start was 4.5 minutes.

The quick reaction alert (QRA) requirement meant added pressure on aircraft and manpower resources. Every time we held the southern QRA duty, two armed aircraft together with a full engineering support team and two pilots were detached day and night to the QRA hangar positioned near the end of the runway. When scrambled, the aircraft could get airborne within two minutes. As soon as one Lightning had departed, the standby aircraft had to be made immediately available just in case the on-task machine returned unserviceable. My SEngO would often put aircraft on QRA duties despite only a few minutes remaining before a 'mandatory service' was due. He followed the principle that the Lightning could be legally airborne on a tanker-supported mission of a couple of hours, giving us enough time to prepare a replacement in addition to counting the hours towards the training task.

As well as not being designed with maintenance in mind, the Lightning was initially meant to be operated from a main operating base in the UK which provided all the technical support facilities necessary to keep the aircraft serviceable and ready to counter the bomber threat. Nevertheless, every operational Lightning squadron was required to demonstrate that it could deploy to, and operate from, NATO bases overseas when required, often at short notice. This presented problems. Although the aircraft did have NATO standard fuel and electrical power connectors, most of the ground-support equipment was not designed for mobility. The staff solution was to provide drawings for various equipment couplings and adaptors to enable our equipment to interface with that of our NATO allies. Needless to say, very little did and thus every time we deployed overseas we were faced with squeezing-in a quart's worth of Lightning kit and spares into a pint-sized transport aircraft. In lighter moments we would wait until the loadmaster of the Hercules transport aircraft was congratulating himself that he had got all the equipment on board and was preparing his trim sheet, then we would tow out a ventral tank on its enormous trolley saying that it had to be loaded! Deployments to warmer climates such as Italy, Malta and Cyprus were always popular with the groundcrew, and even the aircraft showed improved serviceability: hydraulic seals expanded in the heat thereby reducing many oil leaks, furthermore electronic systems performed better as the equipment bays dried out.

Every Lightning squadron was regularly subjected to a lengthy, no-notice tactical evaluation by an experienced team of specialists from Command Headquarters. The taceval team, which often arrived late at night by road so as not to alert the unit, used a series of realistic scenarios to test every aspect of the flying and engineering operations of the squadron to make sure that our procedures were safe and correct. The effectiveness of our call-out plan was usually the first aspect to be put under the taceval microscope. Because there were only a few married quarters at Wattisham, many of the NCOs and technicians lived off base. We had to rely upon a complex 'cascade' notification process to call personnel in and thereby demonstrate that sufficient were available to meet the next phase of the evaluation: aircraft generation. Naturally enough, the initial workload always fell upon the shoulders of those who lived on base and reported in first. Generating sufficient aircraft meant a rapid review of the engineering state board with the servicing team leaders. We had to determine which aircraft could be quickly and safely recovered from scheduled maintenance and defect rectification.

Every step of the generation process was scrutinised by the taceval team who would periodically feed in difficulties to see how we responded. Arming the aircraft with live missiles was always a tense time as it gave the evaluators plenty of opportunities to cause mischief and mayhem as well as making sure that our handling and loading procedures were top notch. This phase enabled the squadron armourers to show how good they were, and fortunately on 29 Squadron we had the best. Evaluating the scramble and flying phases came next, with the pilots being tested on a number of different and demanding attack profiles which involved other Command assets such as bomber targets, fighter escorts and tankers. The engineering task was to carry out operational turn rounds and quickly return the aircraft to the battle and keep it serviceable. This phase was usually interrupted by the taceval team injecting simulated incidents such as aircraft fires, battle damage and weapon problems. The final part of the evaluation was often a survival scramble of all available aircraft to alternative airfields which usually preceded a simulated nuclear attack on Wattisham. Once the last aircraft had roared off into the night sky, I would be struck by the sobering realisation that the engineers, technicians and mechanics were expendable. The important assets were the pilots and the aircraft.

We had lighter moments, too. There was the time that an over-anxious engineering officer, during a night scramble of four aircraft, stumbled into the AC and DC power cables of a Lightning. The cables were pulled out thus preventing the pilot from starting his engines just as he received the order to scramble from the fighter controller. The pilot, flight commander and squadron boss were not amused. I remember watching a young technician on starter crew duties who, as he lay beside his aircraft on a hot and tiring afternoon in Cyprus, promptly jumped to his feet on hearing a starter motor fire up. Then, to the bewilderment of his pilot, he went through the complete starting sequence on his aircraft even though it was the adjacent aircraft that had started up. One of my favourite memories was a hangar incident witnessed by the SEngO and myself. A newly arrived mechanic straight from training saw a Lightning being manoeuvred in the hangar without engines, jet pipes or radar bullet. Suddenly and slowly the aircraft started to tip up on its trolley. Wanting to save the country a few quid, the ten stone airman immediately grabbed the end of the Lightning's pitot tube as ten tons of shiny aircraft continued to rise majestically into the air. When the aircraft finally came to rest on its tail, the young man, his feet now dangling and kicking high in the air, continued to hang on grimly.

The complications of an aircraft design which gave only a passing nod to the maintenance task, coupled with the juggling act of managing spares and manpower shortages, and the relentless pressure of the day and night flying programme, plus exercises, QRA, overseas deployments and tactical evaluations meant that the mechanics, technicians and managers on a Lightning squadron were stretched, if not over-stretched. There seemed to be no pattern to the aircraft defects and every day was different. After only a few sorties an impressive line-up of serviceable aircraft in the morning would often be reduced to none at the end of the day. The night shift would then have to scratch around to generate the minimum number of aircraft required for the next morning's flying programme. Equally, despite an aircraft state board covered in technical graffiti, the technicians and mechanics would work their magic and suddenly, as if from nowhere, serviceable aircraft would appear. No matter how we analysed it, we never fully understood how. Later in my career I went on an air warfare course visit to a United States Air Force fighter base in the UK where we were briefed by the chief of maintenance. Even with his experience he couldn't explain how the serviceability picture could change so quickly either, but he shared a few thoughts which I have always remembered. He said: "Beware the light at the end of the tunnel – it could be the headlights of an oncoming train," and: "If things are going well, find out why." These comments seemed appropriate to my nearly three years as a Lightning squadron engineer.

Despite the problems and difficulties, the engineering task was immensely enjoyable and rewarding. The satisfaction of seeing a line-up of aircraft at the start of a day's flying and watching them depart, usually in fighter pairs, was matched by the run-in and break over the airfield as they returned from a successful training sortie. The best moment for me, however, was to watch the pilot in the line hut after a mission, often hot and fatigued from a demanding sortie, when he wrote the word 'satisfactory' in the aircraft's Form 700 log book, meaning that the aircraft was available for another flight.

And what became of my boss, mentor and life-long friend the SEngO? After he retired from the Royal Air Force, and despite his earlier misgivings, he joined the aerospace company which had produced the Lightning aircraft. He worked in the company's new projects department where, to help design future generations of fighter aircraft, he used lessons hard learned from his Lightning squadron experience. He didn't, however, buy a new smoker's pipe.

APPENDIX A

SELECT BIOGRAPHIES

ROGER COLEBROOK

A 'Baby Boomer' born in 1946, I left school at 16, determined to be an RAF pilot and worked on a farm until I was old enough to join. In 1964 I began an eight-year short-service commission and trained on the Jet Provost (3 FTS 1964-5), Folland Gnat (4 FTS 1965-6), Hawker Hunter (229 OCU 1966), then the Lightning (226 OCU 1966-7).

I joined 56(F) Squadron, Lightning F3, March 1967, based at RAF Wattisham, Suffolk, then RAF Akrotiri, Cyprus. In July 1969 I was posted to CFS for QFI training, but requested a further air-defence tour of duty. I flew the Phantom OCU (700[P] Squadron, RNAS Yeovilton, September 1969) then joined 43(F) Squadron, Phantom FG1, November 1969, based at RAF Leuchars, Fife. In 1972 I decided the air force was not the career for me and took my 'eight-year option' to leave.

For the next 30 years I worked for a number of charter companies including British Caledonian Airways, Air Europe, Korean Air, Air 2000, and EVA Airways of Taiwan operating, amongst others, Beech 18, Piper Aztec, Britten-Norman Trislander, the DC10-30, Boeing 757 and Fokker 100. My final appointment was on the Thomas Cook B757 fleet before I retired in 2006.

DON BROWN

Born in London 1936, and evacuated to Staffordshire during the Blitz where I absorbed an enduring love for open country. I conceived the idea that I would like to be a fighter pilot, while watching wartime news reels of Spitfires shooting down German bombers, thus joined the RAF in 1954 aged 17. I spent the first four years as an air signaller in the Middle East, with 8 Squadron, on the Vickers Valetta. Commenced OTU and pilot training in 1958 and received my wings in 1960.

1961 I flew the Hawker Hunter at Chivenor, then went to 14 Squadron, RAF Germany (NATO) on the Hunter F6 day fighter. 14 Squadron disbanded the following year, and I was posted to 43, Cyprus and later Aden, Middle East Air Force. I returned to the UK in 1965 on the Lightning Conversion Course, Coltishall and joined 74 Squadron, Fighter Command, flying the Lightning F Mk 3, QRA, in air defence of the United Kingdom.

In 1966 I retired from the RAF and flew Lightnings/Hunters for the Royal Saudi Air Force, as a display pilot. (Operation Magic Carpet.) From 1967 to 1992 I flew with Qantas Airways in Sydney (Boeing 707, 747, 747 – 400), ultimately as training captain, retiring in 1996 at the flying age limit of 60. From there I took up civilian posts for Cathay and QANTAS and now live in the Southern Highlands of New South Wales where I play with my Classic cars, tend my garden, and watch my offspring's careers with interest.

ALAN WINKLES

I was born in Torquay, Devon and became a member of the Air Training Corps at school. At 17 I gained my pilot's licence on Tiger Moths and joined the RAF a year later to become a fighter pilot. My first appointment in 1966 was as a Lightning Air Defence pilot on 5 Squadron at RAF Binbrook. After this three-year tour I transferred to the newly-arrived Phantom and became a qualified weapons instructor serving on 54 Squadron at RAF Coningsby and then on 17 Squadron at RAF Bruggen. In 1973 I became a flight commander on 43 Squadron (Phantoms) at RAF Leuchars. I then commanded the Royal Navy's Phantom training squadron and spent six months with 892 Naval Air Squadron on HMS *Ark Royal*.

After a tour on the weapons staff at HQ 38 Group RAF Upavon, I attended Staff College at RAF Bracknell and was posted to army staff duties at the MOD London. Following promotion I took up duties as wing commander training at HQ 11 Group at RAF Bentley Priory. From there I was posted to assume command of 43 Squadron (Phantoms) at RAF Leuchars.

In 1987 I was posted to the Sultan of Oman's air force but in 1990 I returned to the RAF Staff College as a member of the directing staff. In 1993 I went to HQ US CENTCOM at MacDill Air Force Base in Tampa, Florida as the first and sole British exchange officer. From here I was posted to the Defence Evaluation and Research Agency (now QinetiQ) at Malvern in January 1996, retiring from the RAF in July 2001.

I have flown more than 5,000 hours mainly in fighters. In retirement I became an A2 flying instructor with the Air Training Corps flying Vigilant (Grob 109) motor gliders and sending dozens of 16-year-old cadets solo. I also enjoy conventional gliding.

TERRY DAVIES

Born in the West Country, the son of an RAF warrant officer, I attended schools in Somerset, the Isle of Man, West Germany, Southampton and Wallingford. I joined the RAF as a university cadet whilst studying physics and mathematics at London University. Engineer officer training at RAF College Cranwell was followed by my first tour as junior engineer officer on 29(F) Squadron, RAF Wattisham, equipped with the Lightning F Mk 3. Further command and staff appointments followed including Lightning tours at RAF Wattisham as OC Electrical Engineering Squadron and in Riyadh, Saudi Arabia as the electrical engineering specialist with the first MOD team. Following Staff College I was posted to RAF Finningley as OC Engineering Wing and then to Washington DC as the F4 Phantom liaison officer with the United States Navy. On returning to the UK I attended the Air Warfare Course at Cranwell followed by Ministry of Defence appointments in London and NATO posts in Munich on the Tornado.

After two-and-a-half years as a first-tour Lightning engineer, everything that followed seemed easy!

ROGER BEAZLEY

I only flew the one tour on the Lightning, based at RAF Gütersloh in Germany with 19(F) Squadron; fondly remembered now as a most agreeable and formative three years. Following a further three years flying Phantoms with 43(F) Squadron at RAF Leuchars in Scotland I attended the Empire Test Pilots' School (ETPS) at Boscombe Down. The majority of my RAF career was then spent in the flight test and flight research business retiring from the service in 1996. I subsequently completed 12 years civilian employment as a full-time consultant and aerospace adviser in flight test and associated activities. I was awarded an AFC in 1978 and appointed CBE in 1996. Now fully retired, I am very much involved in the flying supervision of a number of air displays both in the UK and overseas, and continue to fly light aircraft.

SIMON MORRIS

I was brought up in Tanzania, formerly Tanganyika, East Africa and joined the

RAF in 1970. After training on the Hunter aircraft I was posted to the Lightning in May 1973. I served on 92 Squadron based at RAF Gütersloh in West Germany from August '73 until the Lightnings were disbanded in April 1977. During my time on 92 Squadron I wrote the squadron history using the diaries and official records. This can be seen online at http://www.92squadron.com.

After the RAF I served in Singapore and Saudi Arabia before joining British Airways, retiring as a captain on the Boeing 777. I now live in Northern Thailand.

DR RICHARD MARSH

I was born in 1944 and educated in my home town of Cambridge and then London. Today I am a chartered engineer, a fellow of the Institution of Mechanical Engineers, and a fellow of the Institution of Electrical Engineers and a Doctor of Technology.

At the age of 22 my career began as a graduate apprentice and then a mechanical and aeronautical engineer on the Concorde design team with The British Aircraft Corporation in Bristol. It took twelve years to complete and get sixteen aircraft into service. I then transferred within the company to the Guided Weapons Division where we created one of the world's first remotely-operated submarines. This brought me to Aberdeen where I established my first company in 1979, and my second in 1991. Both companies specialised in the design, production and international marketing of high technology subsea electronic and robotic products. The second, Tritech International Ltd., became the most highly-decorated company in the North Sea oil industry winning Queens Awards and several other significant industry accolades. Both companies were sold to UK PLCs and I now work from home helping young engineers start their own company.

MARCUS WILLS

I graduated from Cranwell in July 1964 having flown the Chipmunk and Jet Provost, before moving on to Valley, Chivenor and Coltishall to fly the Gnat, Hunter and Lightning. I joined 111 Squadron in January 1966 and sadly completed only one two-and-a-half-year tour before being posted as ADC to the air officer commanding-in-chief Air Support Command – a tour which gave me my first taste of the worldwide and excitingly varied role of the transport fleet. I joined 10 Squadron in 1971 to fly VC10s, first as a co-pilot before promotion to captain, flight commander and finally, after the requisite dose of Staff College and ground tour, commanded the squadron. Some 4,000 flying hours on the VC10 included flights with HM The Queen, other members of the royal family and four successive prime ministers from Heath to Thatcher – tasks which continued when I became station commander at Benson and deputy captain of The Queen's Flight in 1984. There are many stories from these latter tours that may one day be told, but for the time being – and I am sure that many other contributors to this book will agree – our adventures on the Lightning take some beating!

SIR JOSEPH GILBERT KCB CBE

I learned to fly with my University Air Squadron and within a year had joined 1 Squadron flying Meteors at Tangmere in 1953. My flying career encompassed commands of a flight, a squadron, a group and I finished as deputy commander Allied Forces Central Europe. Between flying tours, I served in policy staff posts in Whitehall and NATO.

After leaving the service, I have been president of the RAF Association, trustee of the Imperial War Museum and chairman of the Commonwealth War Graves Commission. I'm now deep in retirement but act as a guide in Salisbury Cathedral. My favourite aircraft is unsurprisingly the Lightning!

ALASTAIR (ALI) McKAY

I have had a varied career in both the military and retail. I joined the RAF in 1964 as a cadet at the RAF College Cranwell and retired as a group captain in 1989. During that time I flew the Lightning and Phantom aircraft. I commanded 56(F) Squadron at RAF Wattisham from 1984 to 1986 and was station commander RAF Wildenrath in Germany from 1987 to 1989.

I joined the John Lewis Partnership in January 1990 as a senior management trainee and spent my first year in various appointments within the Department Store Division. In January 1991 I joined the Board of Waitrose as director of Retail Operations and was responsible for the development, trading activity and management of all the Waitrose shops. In 2000 I joined the main Partnership Board in the post of Partners' Counsellor (Ombudsman) and in 2003 became director of Corporate Responsibility where tasks included CSR, intelligence, business continuity and all aspects of corporate governance. For my last two years in the Partnership, I was deputy chairman. I retired from the Partnership in February 2007 and am now involved in trustee work associated with two charities in small business development.

INDEX

Aircraft

Miscellaneous